Great moments in the history of the Jewish people, told in fascinating comic-cartoon story-strips, with descriptive background information accompanying each true adventure

A PICTURE PARADE
OF JEWISH HISTORY

By MORRIS EPSTEIN

Illustrated by MAURICE del BOURGO *and* F. L. BLAKE

BLOCH PUBLISHING COMPANY, INC.

New York

ISBN 0-8197-0024-X   LIBRARY OF CONGRESS CATALOG CARD NUMBER 63-13317

Text: Copyright 1963 by Morris Epstein. Illustrations: Copyright 1963 by Maurice del Bourgo and F. L. Blake. Printed in the United States of America.

CONTENTS:

INTRODUCTION

During one of New York's periodic newspaper strikes, the late Mayor Fiorello H. La Guardia rushed to a radio microphone to perform an unusual public service. Realizing that a great metropolis was hungry for news, he dramatically met the crisis.

Did he fill the vacuum with the latest headlines? International developments? Municipal events? No. He read the comics, and thus satisfied a yearning keenly felt by his fellow citizens.

Today, as in La Guardia's time, the comics are a daily American habit. They are read by 80 million youngsters and grownups across the nation, and close to 200 comic magazines achieve a monthly circulation of over 60 million copies. They have defied movies and television and claims from abroad that the United States was being destroyed from within by comic books.

Was there ever a time when there were no cartoon strips? It's hard to believe it, but the answer is yes. Comics were born in 1896 when Joseph Pulitzer's *New York World* presented a smiling little boy with a bald head and flap ears dressed in a yellow nightgown who was a cartoon comment on slum life in the big city.

"Look at the 'Yellow Kid'!" cried the readers, and the adjective leaped from the cartoon panel to become half of the famous phrase, "yellow journalism," a label applied to sensational newspaper practices of that era.

Trends and fashions changed, but comics were here to stay. Slapstick remained a staple, but the field spread out to include adventure, space travel, sports, animal lore, science, and, most recently, humor so sophisticated that it is a sign of status to admire it.

When feverish expansion led to excesses in horror and crime cartoons, comic-book publishers stilled protests by setting up a self-regulating organization with a strict code of rules.

Regulated or not, comics continued to thrive. They are easy to read, easy to understand. They have color and immediacy. They portray a world of heroes in which the bad are punished and the good rewarded.

Used properly, they can instruct as well as entertain. Public agencies have begun to harness cartoon-power for worthwhile purposes. The Police Department in New York City has just published a million cartoon-strip books in a campaign to persuade children to respect the law. Civil defense workers have been recruited through comics. And political aspirants, from local to Presidential level, both egghead and lowbrow, have resorted to coaxing by comic.

That brings us to this book. But first a word from Al Capp. The creator of *Li'l Abner* once said, "If comics can sharpen the taste for cereal or spinach, they can certainly be used to awaken an interest in music, literature, and good living. If Abner listens to a Mozart symphony instead of to cheap, maudlin songs, without intruding into the basic idea of the comic as entertainment, 100,000 kids may want to hear what that symphony sounds like."

Now what is true for a Mozart symphony is equally valid for an opera, a good book, an ethical approach to life. One more step and the premise of the present book is established. For Jewish history offers a fascinating roster of heroes acting out an exciting drama of peoplehood. If these cartoon stories introduce children to famous faces, places, dates, and happenings; if the ready accessibility of the background texts increases their chance of being read; if a pleasant sense of familiarity is aroused when the cast of characters is encountered in more formal study, an author's fond hopes will have been fulfilled.

Behind the words in this book lies the research of many scholars, and I thank the historians for their silent assistance. I wrote a number of the cartoon strips, but none of the background texts, originally for *World Over,* the children's magazine published by the Jewish Education Committee, and I am grateful to Dr. Azriel Eisenberg, the Committee's executive vice-president, for facilitating reprint arrangements. My sincere thanks are extended to my colleague, Ezekiel Schloss, who supervised the art preparation of those cartoons which appeared in *World Over.*

Moshe Sheinbaum, president of Shengold Publishers, was always helpful, stimulating, and cooperative, and Maurice del Bourgo and F. L. Blake, artists and gentlemen both, whipped through time and space with the effortless ease of Superman. The felicity of the illustrations is theirs; any errors in text are mine.

I owe more than words can express to the warm encouragement and discerning taste of my wife Shifra. Finally, I have reached the proud moment when I can thank our children, Guita and Sherry. For the first time they have been first readers of a book their father has written for them and for children everywhere.

January, 1963   MORRIS EPSTEIN

THE SEPTUAGINT

A COMMITTEE of Jewish scholars is now preparing the first modern English translation of the Bible directly from the traditional Hebrew text. The authorities working on this twenty-year project are the latest successors to those seventy who, twenty-two centuries ago, it is said, produced the "Septuagint"—the Translation of the Seventy.

In both cases the reason for the translation is the same. It is to make the treasures of the Bible available to those who cannot read it in Hebrew.

Alexandria, Egypt, founded by Alexander the Great of Macedonia in 331 B.C.E., was the first Greek-ruled city to give citizenship to Jews. Under the rule of the Ptolemy kings who followed Alexander, the Jewish community prospered. Its members spoke Greek and admired Greek culture. They read Greek books and studied Greek ideas.

They began to lose the knowledge of Hebrew, and were faced with the danger of losing their relationship with Judaism. They met this problem by teaching their children Hebrew and by translating the Pentateuch—the Five Books of Moses—into Greek, so that the spirit of their heritage might remain with them.

The Jews of Egypt wove a legend about this translation. In a book by one Aristeas of Alexandria it is written that Ptolemy II, who ruled between 285 and 247 B.C.E., wanted to have the best library in the world. His librarian reported to him that he already had 995 great books, but that the five finest books of all were not his collection. These books, he said, were the Five Books of Moses.

Impressed, the king sent ambassadors to Jerusalem. They asked the high priest for a copy of these books and for men who could translate them into Greek. Whereupon a copy of the Torah was sent to Alexandria, accompanied by seventy-two learned scribes.

The king received the guests with great honor and marveled at their wisdom. When the welcoming festivities were over, he placed each scholar in a separate room, and asked each to translate the Torah by himself.

The seventy-two scholars were done in seventy-two days, and the versions were then compared. Lo, all the translations were exactly alike in every word and letter! So proud was everyone that a holiday was declared, to be observed each year in honor of the completion of the Septuagint.

From the Septuagint came translations of the Bible into other languages. The *legend* of how it was made is interesting; the *fact,* namely, that the Septuagint helped bring the Book of Books to the entire world, is even more fascinating.

8

TRANSLATION OF THE SEVENTY

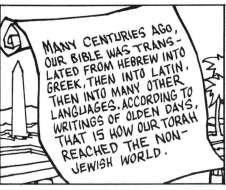

MANY CENTURIES AGO, OUR BIBLE WAS TRANSLATED FROM HEBREW INTO GREEK, THEN INTO LATIN, THEN INTO MANY OTHER LANGUAGES. ACCORDING TO WRITINGS OF OLDEN DAYS, THAT IS HOW OUR TORAH REACHED THE NON-JEWISH WORLD.

IN EGYPT, LONG AGO.

I, KING PTOLEMY, HAVE HEARD THE JEWS POSSESS AN EXCELLENT BOOK. THEY CALL IT THE TORAH. I WILL HAVE A GREEK TRANSLATION MADE!

ARISTEAS! TAKE COSTLY GIFTS TO JERUSALEM! BRING BACK 70 WISE MEN WHO UNDERSTAND THE TORAH!

ARISTEAS DELIVERED HIS MESSAGE TO ELEAZAR, THE HIGH PRIEST, IN JERUSALEM.

BE MY GUEST WHILE I CHOOSE 70 OF OUR GREATEST SAGES.

AT LAST, THEY WERE ASSEMBLED. THEY GO ONLY BECAUSE OF THE GREAT BLESSING THAT THE TRANSLATION OF THE TORAH CAN BRING. SHALOM!

THEY ARRIVED IN ALEXANDRIA.

WELCOME, SAGES! TONIGHT -- A BANQUET; TOMORROW -- TO YOUR HOLY TASK!

PTOLEMY TESTED THE WISDOM OF THE 70 SAGES.

WHAT'S MOST DIFFICULT FOR A KING?

-TO MASTER HIMSELF.

TO WHOM SHALL WE DO GOOD?

FIRST TO OUR PARENTS, THEN TO OUR FELLOW-MEN.

THE FOLLOWING DAY, ON AN ISLAND OUTSIDE THE CITY.

HERE ARE 70 HOUSES, ONE FOR EACH OF YOU. YOU WILL HAVE FOOD AND SERVANTS.

EACH OF YOU WILL TRANSLATE THE TORAH INTO GREEK. FAREWELL!

I WILL KNOW THE TRANSLATION IS CORRECT IF ALL VERSIONS OF THE 70 SAGES READ ALIKE!

AFTER 70 DAYS THE 70 SAGES APPEARED BEFORE THE KING.

WE HAVE COMPLETED OUR TRANSLATIONS.

AND ALL OF THEM AGREE.. IN EVERY WAY!

LET THIS TRANSLATION BE FOREVER KNOWN THE SEPTUAGINT -- THE "TRANSLATION OF THE 70!"

THUS, IT IS WRITTEN, WAS MADE THE FIRST TRANSLATION OF OUR TORAH. THROUGH THE SEPTUAGINT, IT REACHED THE WIDE WIDE WORLD.

HILLEL

THOSE who lived in the period before the destruction of the Second Temple conducted themselves as if they knew of the tragedy that awaited Judea. In the lands of exile, Jews created a life of the spirit; with the Bible as their portable homeland, they built flourishing communities in Babylonia, Egypt, and Syria.

Within the boundaries of the Holy Land the Temple became a symbol of unity. Three times a year, Jerusalem and its suburbs would be dotted with tents as hundreds of thousands of visitors made their pilgrimage for the festivals of Passover, Shavuot, and Sukkot. The Synagogue was established, and slowly it developed into a house of prayer, of study, and of assembly.

As if they knew that their survival would one day depend on study, the people concentrated on education, which they considered as important as prayer. The Bible said, "You shall teach these words to your children," and Jewish sages added, *Talmud Torah k'neged kulam*: "Most important of all is the study of Torah."

Of Judea's many teachers, the most noted were Shammai and Hillel, who lived in the 1st century B.C.E. They were friendly rivals, as different in personality as two human beings could be. Shammai was stern, strict, and easily irritated. Hillel was even-tempered, kind, and patient.

Born and trained in Babylonia, Hillel was drawn to Jerusalem by the reputation of its scholars. There he continued his studies, until he became the head of a renowned academy and the leader of the Sanhedrin.

Hillel's wisdom is revealed in the famous story about a heathen who tried to ridicule Judaism. This man, who did not believe in God, said to Shammai that he would become a Jew if Shammai could teach him the Torah while the student stood on one leg without tiring. Shammai angrily threw him out and he came to Hillel, who cheerfully undertook the assignment. Basing his answer on the Bible's command to "love your neighbor as yourself," he said, "What is hateful to you, do not do to another. This is the whole Torah; the rest only explains this law." According to the story, the heathen was so impressed that he became a Jew.

Many other wise sayings of Hillel have come down to us. Here are a few:

"Do not judge your neighbor until you know what it is like to be in his place."

"Do not separate yourself from the community."

"Reviewing a lesson 100 times cannot be compared with reviewing it 101 times."

Hillel's warm approach to cold law won everyone's heart. After his death, his name stood for an ideal combination of scholarship and kindliness, of deep thought and simple devotion to God.

10

SNOW ON THE ROOF

YOHANAN BEN ZAKKAI

THE founder of the famous academy of learning in Yavneh was a pupil of great teachers and a teacher of renowned students.

He studied at the feet of the famed sages Hillel and Shammai, and his pupils included Eliezer ben Hyrcanus, Joshua ben Hananiah, Eliezer ben Arach, and others.

His life spanned a century of important events. According to tradition he was born in 40 B.C.E. and died in 80 C.E., thus living a full 120 years.

He witnessed the destruction of the Second Temple and, by creating the academy at Yavneh, he passed the torch of Torah to future generations.

As a member of the Great Sanhedrin in Jerusalem, Yohanan ben Zakkai foresaw that Rome would conquer Judea. When the Roman General Vespasian started the siege of Jerusalem in the year 68 C.E., Yohanan wished to yield, so that unnecessary bloodshed might be avoided and his request for an academy of learning might be granted.

He could not obtain permission to leave the city and the story is told that he pretended to be dead and had himself carried out in a coffin.

The city which Yohanan ben Zakkai asked of Vespasian is on the Mediterranean coast between Jaffa and Ashdod. Yohanan ben Zakkai found it a well-populated, well-fortified city. He gathered about him a small community of sages and organized the academy which he had planned.

When the terrible news reached Yavneh that the Temple in Jerusalem lay in ashes, the aging teacher tore his garments, and his disciples wept. But he followed mourning with action, re-creating a new Sanhedrin, or Supreme Court, and establishing laws and regulations which had a lasting influence on Jewish life.

Yohanan ben Zakkai was a man of deep wisdom and humility. One of his favorite sayings was: "If you have learned much Torah, do not ask for praise, for you were created to study."

It is said that he never permitted anyone to greet him first, not even a slave whom he met on the street. What is more, "in all his days he never uttered idle words." He was beloved by all and "no one ever opened the door of the school for his pupils except Yohanan ben Zakkai himself."

These are but a few of many sayings which have come down to this day. They have survived because Yohanan ben Zakkai was so noted for his scholarship and devotion to the Law that he was a very highly regarded figure in Jewish history.

But of all his accomplishments his greatest was Yavneh. His foresight and determination helped adjust Jewish life to an existence without a Temple in Jerusalem. He made Yavneh the symbol of Jewish spiritual survival.

12

'GIVE ME YAVNEH'

AKIBA

AKIBA BEN JOSEPH, who began to study as a grown man those things which any child knew, would one day be the greatest scholar in the scholars' city of Yavneh.

His years of study meant years of painful separation from his dear wife. Rachel did not complain, but worked harder than ever to support their family, while she nourished the hope that some day her husband would be a brilliant sage in Israel.

It is said that when Akiba returned home he was followed by thousands of pupils. His wife came out to meet him. His students had never seen her and did not know who she was. Thinking she was a rude stranger, they tried to push her aside. But Rabbi Akiba welcomed her and said to his students: "Be gracious to her. Your wisdom, as well as mine, is due to her." And in reward for Rachel's sacrifices, he presented her with a golden crown engraved with a picture of Jerusalem.

Akiba, who lived about 50 to 135 C.E., was to play the double role of rabbi and rebel. He gathered and arranged the teachings of many earlier rabbis. Each academy of learning had added laws when they were needed. Akiba divided all Jewish law into six large areas. In doing so, he prepared the way for the huge task of compiling the Mishnah, a labor to be completed by Judah Ha-Nasi.

His brilliance was matched by his modesty. He said, "Always take a place lower than you deserve until you are asked to occupy a higher one. It is better to be asked to come up than to be told to step down."

Rabbi Akiba journeyed to Arabia and Asia and North Africa, meeting with his people in exile. During all this time, he cherished the dream that his beloved Judea would one day throw off the yoke of foreign rule. When Bar Kochba presented himself and said he was ready to rise against the cruel Romans, Rabbi Akiba became an inspired rebel.

The rebellion did not succeed and the Romans avenged themselves by striking at the heart of Jewish life. They forbade the practice of all Jewish customs. Old and weary, Akiba defied the Romans and continued to teach the Torah. He knew that teachers were being hunted down for passing on to their students the Torah's lessons. He knew that rabbis were being thrown into chains for ordaining their pupils as rabbis.

The blow fell. Ten scholars were chosen by the Roman Emperor Hadrian to be put to death for disobeying the imperial order. One of them was Rabbi Akiba. He was about 80 when he went fearlessly to the stake. As he was being tortured, he proclaimed the *Shema*: "Hear, O Israel, the Lord our God, the Lord is One." These were his last words.

In the centuries that followed, the name of Akiba became a synonym for bravery and martyrdom.

14

DROPS OF WATER

BAR KOCHBA

MORE than half a century had passed since Titus had destroyed the Temple in 70 C.E. and led Jewish captives across the sea to Rome.

The Jews who remained in the wasteland of Zion resigned themselves to waiting for deliverance, though their hearts told them it was in vain.

But there was one who refused to sit by idly. Rabbi Akiba, now aged and weary, taught the Torah despite the Roman decree against religious study; told the fearful ones that, as a fish could not live without water, so could the Jewish people not exist without Torah.

One day there came to Rabbi Akiba a mighty man, fierce-looking and broad-shouldered. "I am Simeon bar Koziba," he said. "I stand ready to strike the blow of vengeance!"

Akiba said, "In the Bible it is written: 'There shall step forth a star out of Jacob and destroy the enemies of Israel.' I name you Bar Kochba—Son of the Star!"

Thousands of followers were drawn to the new leader. They even came from communities outside of Judea. Under Bar Kochba's guidance, the people prepared secretly, hiding their homemade weapons in caves and ravines against the day of revenge.

The moment came soon enough. In Rome, Emperor Hadrian ordered his Judean governor to erect a pagan temple in Jerusalem. Bar Kochba moved swiftly. In two years, his men captured ninety forts and a thousand cities and villages, including Jerusalem.

Frightened lest other enslaved peoples follow Bar Kochba's example, Hadrian sent his best general, Julius Severus, into the fray. Severus retook all the forts, and Bar Kochba was forced to retreat to the mountain stronghold of Betar in the Judean hills near Jerusalem.

For one whole year the Romans laid siege to the city. At last, on the Ninth of Av in 135 C.E., they broke through the gates and poured into Betar. Bar Kochba fought grimly to the end, and fell sword in hand; Rabbi Akiba was put to a cruel death by the Roman governor.

Ancient documents and coins, even now being discovered in Israel, are witness to the historic revolt. Military orders from Bar Kochba to a deputy have come to light, and minted coins bearing the words "For the freedom of Jerusalem," and requests for palm branches and citrons for the Festival of Tabernacles in the year 134. Bar Kochba did all that was humanly possible to keep alive the flame of rebellion against tyranny.

But it was snuffed out. Half a million Jews died in the year 135. The defeat of Judea was complete, but the exploits of Bar Kochba remained forever inscribed in the chronicles of Jewish history.

16

THE FALL OF BETAR

JERUSALEM WAS IN RUINS AND THE TEMPLE WAS BUT A HEAP OF STONES SACKED BY TITUS THE ROMAN...

60 YEARS HAD PASSED SINCE TITUS THE ROMAN HAD SACKED THE TEMPLE, WHEN THERE AROSE A MAN...

RABBI AKIBA, I HAVE COME TO LEAD MY PEOPLE OUT OF ROMAN BONDAGE!

AKIBA SAW THAT THIS MAN'S SPIRIT WAS A FLAME...

THE BIBLE SAYS: "THERE SHALL COME A STAR (KOCHAV) OUT OF JACOB!" I NAME YOU BAR KOCHBA!

24,000 DISCIPLES OF RABBI AKIBA TURNED TO BAR KOCHBA.

LEAD US, BAR KOCHBA!

THE ENEMY IS MIGHTY. I MUST TEST EACH OF YOU, TO JUDGE YOUR STRENGTH!

TO PASS THE TEST, EACH MAN HAD TO UPROOT A CEDAR ON HORSE-BACK!

BAR KOCHBA HARASSED THE ENEMY ON EVERY SIDE.

A VICTORY FOR BAR KOCHBA!

IN ROME, EMPEROR HADRIAN WAS FRIGHTENED BY THE REVOLT IN JUDEA.

JULIUS SEVERUS, YOU ARE MY GREAT-EST GENERAL. TAKE 4 LEGIONS AND DEFEAT BAR KOCHBA!

CUNNINGLY, SEVERUS DECIDED TO STARVE THE JEWS.

CHOKE UP THE WELLS! CUT OFF THE SUPPLY ROADS!

BAR KOCHBA RETREATED TO THE LAST STRONGHOLD: BETAR IN THE JUDEAN HILLS. TIME PASSED.

BAR KOCHBA, WE'VE BEEN ONE YEAR WITHOUT FOOD! MEN ARE DYING IN THE STREETS!

AT LAST THE ROMANS BROKE THROUGH...

BETTER DEATH AS FREE MEN, THAN LIFE AS SLAVES UNDER THE ROMANS!

ON THE 9TH OF AV, 135 C.E., BAR KOCHBA FELL...

...BUT HIS REVOLT BECAME A LIVING SYM-BOL OF OUR PEOPLE'S DESIRE FOR FREE-DOM AND INDEPENDENCE!

JUDAH HA-NASI

18

THE basic textbook of Jewish law and thought after the Bible is the Mishnah. In its six volumes are gathered all the laws which had been taught orally by teachers to their students for centuries. The man whose life work consisted of editing, compiling, and classifying this body of law was Rabbi Judah Ha-Nasi.

"Ha-Nasi" means "the Prince." Rabbi Judah is also called *"Rabenu Ha-Kadosh"* (our holy teacher). These titles show what an impression he made on those who knew him.

According to tradition, he was born on the day Rabbi Akiba died in 135 C.E. This coincidence was taken to symbolize the unbroken chain of Jewish learning. A descendant of Hillel, he succeeded his father, Rabbi Gamaliel II, as head of the Sanhedrin.

He was also the political leader of the Palestinian Jewish community. The Temple was gone, and close relations had to be maintained with the Roman authorities. They respected Judah the Prince for his wisdom and for the dignity with which he conducted himself.

A wealthy man, he distributed his funds freely to the poor. His main interests were in study and in his beloved pupils. "I learned much from my teachers," he once said, "much more from my comrades, and most of all from my students." His greatest achievement was the preparation of the Mishnah. With the help of his pupils and colleagues, he completed the task about the year 200 C.E.

The Mishnah is written in Hebrew, for Judah loved the Holy Tongue and insisted on speaking only Hebrew with his family and friends despite the fact that Aramaic was then the common language of the Jewish people.

In its final form the Mishnah consists of six sections, or orders. The six sections, known as Sedarim, are divided into sixty-three tractates or treatises; each treatise is subdivided into chapters and each chapter is further subdivided into paragraphs.

Each order of the Mishnah deals with a large area of Jewish life, such as Festivals, Civil and Criminal Law, Laws of Agriculture, and so on.

Although the Mishnah consists mainly of laws, it occasionally presents a story or a wise saying of a rabbi. It also contains a section called *Ethics of the Fathers,* in which are gathered wonderful teachings of the rabbis concerning honest living and proper behavior.

Judah Ha-Nasi died shortly after the Mishnah was done. He was the last of the Tannaim, the teachers and rabbis of the first two centuries who participated in the development of the Mishnah, and his death brought to a close a great period of Jewish scholarship.

THE PRINCE

SOLOMON IBN GABIROL

IN the year 711 Mohammed's followers crossed the Strait of Gibraltar and overran Spain. In doing so, they released from persecution a whole Jewish community. Spanish Jewry grew in numbers and in strength. Spain saw a Jewish cultural development so rich that the period became known as the Golden Age of Spain.

One young poet who was a product of the Golden Age, a sensitive soul whose childhood was unhappy and whose flowering was brief but brilliant, was Solomon ibn Gabirol. He was born in Malaga, Spain, in 1021, and was orphaned before he had reached his teens. He felt lonely and unwanted, and his restlesssness found an outlet in wandering from city to city.

By the time he was 16, he had already begun to express his innermost feelings in tender, pessimistic poems. He felt at home with poetry, and he once wrote, "I am the master, and song is a slave to me."

He was barely 20 when he wrote a Hebrew book of grammar consisting of 400 verses, in which he not only gave the rules of grammar but chided his people for neglecting the holy tongue.

Solomon loved Hebrew and that love makes his religious poems shimmer with beauty and deep emotion. In one poem, he speaks of God as a pillar of strength in time of distress:

In trembling and fear I have made
  Thee my tower;
I look for no aid but Thy strength
  and Thy power.

Some of his poems were so widely known that they were included in prayer books and are still recited in synagogues throughout the world.

Solomon ibn Gabirol's keen mind found another avenue of expression in philosophy. One of his works, *The Fountain of Life,* had a strange history. Written in Arabic, it explained the teachings of early Greek scholars. It was very popular and was translated into Spanish and later into Latin. For hundreds of years it was studied by Christian philosophers, who thought it had been written by someone called Avicebron.

In the 19th century, a man named Solomon Munk was working in the National Library in Paris. He found part of the original Arabic of *The Fountain of Life.* Comparing it with its Latin translation, *Fons Vitae,* he discovered that both were the same. It had taken 800 years to learn that ibn Gabirol was the real author.

Solomon ibn Gabirol's sad and solitary life was brought to an early close. He died in 1058 at the age of 37. He had only had time to sing a few songs, but each was a gem that captured the heart of his people.

20

THE POET-PHILOSOPHER

RASHI

22

BORN in 1040 in Troyes, in northeast France, Rabbi Solomon ben Isaac, or Rashi, wrote historic commentaries on nearly all the books of the Bible and on most of the Talmud.

After studying in the Rhineland, Rashi (an abbreviation of "*R*abbi *Sh*lomo *I*tzhaki") returned to his native city. At the age of 25 he became a rabbi in Troyes and founded a talmudical academy there. His school rapidly won a wide reputation. Students came to him from distant places. Many questions on Jewish law were addressed to him and his decisions were preserved in the works of his pupils.

In his time, the Jews of France lived in friendship with their Christian neighbors. Many of them owned fields and vineyards, while others raised cattle or were traders.

. Rashi, too, owned a vineyard. It is likely that he earned his livelihood by the making of wine. He had three daughters, all of whom married noted rabbis, and many scholars were to be among his descendants.

It was while teaching his students that Rashi began to jot down his explanations of difficult words and passages. In teaching Talmud, Rashi saw that the lack of good commentaries, added to the absence of punctuation, was making this vast sea of laws, customs, and folklore a locked treasure-house.

His commentaries on the Talmud and Bible soon became a necessary tool to their study. So popular was Rashi's work that his commentary on the Five Books of Moses was selected in 1475 as the first Hebrew book ever to be printed.

Because "square" letters were reserved for the Bible, Talmud, and prayer books, the printers used special type for the commentary. This type was later known as "rabbinic" or "Rashi" script.

His commentaries were loved because of their simple, brief, and exact style. Very often he quoted the French translation of a rare Hebrew word. These notes later proved valuable for the study of medieval French and its pronunciation. Rashi's name was paired with the Bible. People spoke of studying "Humash (Five Books of Moses) and Rashi."

The fame of Rashi soon spread beyond the boundaries of France and the German provinces of the Rhine. Jewish and Christian scholars alike began to use Rashi's commentaries. They were translated into Latin, German, English, and many other languages. And over a hundred commentaries have been written on Rashi's own work.

Most important, he helped to bring an ancient heritage to the Jewish people as a whole. He showed that Jewish learning was meaningful not for an age but for every generation.

He died in 1105. He holds such a high place in Jewish tradition that the name "Rashi" has been interpreted as the initials of "*R*abban *sh*el *I*srael," the teacher of Israel.

THE GREAT COMMENTATOR

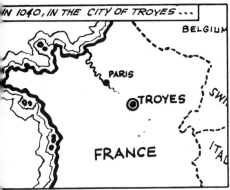

IN 1040, IN THE CITY OF TROYES...

BELGIUM

PARIS

TROYES

FRANCE

RABBI ISAAC, YOUR WIFE HAS GIVEN BIRTH TO A BOY!

YOUR NAME WILL BE SHLOMO. MAY YOU GROW UP TO BE A LEARNED MAN.

MAZEL TOV!

GOOD HEALTH!

MAY GOD BLESS HIM!

RABBI ISAAC COULD NOT HAVE DREAMT THAT HIS SON'S NAME WOULD LIVE AMONG THE JEWISH PEOPLE, WITH GREAT HONOR, FOR EVER AND EVER.

AS A BOY, SHLOMO STUDIED THE BIBLE AND TALMUD.

FATHER, THERE ARE SO MANY HARD PASSAGES HERE.

TRUE, MY SON. WE DO THE BEST WE CAN.

SHLOMO FELT THAT NOT ENOUGH PEOPLE UNDERSTOOD THE BIBLE. STUDYING, HE TOOK NOTES.

I WILL EXPLAIN THE BIBLE... AND THEN THE TALMUD...

IN 1475, HIS BIBLE COMMENTARY WAS CHOSEN TO BE THE FIRST HEBREW BOOK TO BE PRINTED. HERE IS PART OF THE LAST PAGE OF THAT BOOK, IN THE TYPE LATER CALLED "RASHI SCRIPT."

RASHI WROTE A COMMENTARY ON EVERY BOOK OF THE BIBLE EXCEPT CHRONICLES. THEN HE TURNED TO THE TALMUD.

WHERE ARE YOU GOING, MY HUSBAND?

I MUST LEARN ALL ABOUT THE TRADES AND PROFESSIONS IN THE TALMUD.

HE STUDIED MEDICINE, SHOE-MAKING, SHIP-CONSTRUCTION - SO THAT HE COULD FATHOM THE RICHES OF THE TALMUD.

DOES IT INJURE THE HORSE WHEN YOU NAIL ON THE SHOE?

NOT IF YOU DO IT PROPERLY. I'LL SHOW YOU...

THE RABBIS OF THE MIDDLE AGES CALLED RASHI "PARSHANDATA" -- INTERPRETER OF THE LAW. FROM NEAR AND FAR THEY CAME TO STUDY UNDER HIM.

ON THE 29th OF TAMMUZ, 1105, RASHI DIED. HIS NAME LIVED ON - FOR JEWS EVERYWHERE HAVE SINCE SPOKEN OF HUMASH AND RASHI - THE HOLY BIBLE AND RASHI.

AND NOW LET US SEE WHAT RASHI SAYS ABOUT THIS PASSAGE

RASHI BECAME ONE OF THE MOST REVERED PERSONALITIES IN JEWISH HISTORY... RARELY HAD THE WORLD SEEN A MAN OF HIS WISDOM AND LEARNING BEFORE; RARELY WOULD IT SEE HIS LIKE AGAIN.

JUDAH HA-LEVI

IT occasionally happens that a man and his time form a perfect union. Genius, born in the right age, readily prospers. Shakespeare is a case in point, for this unequalled writer of plays lived in a period which appreciated exciting poetic speech.

Still another example is Judah Ha-Levi.

In the glorious procession of Jewish statesmen, scholars, scientists, and explorers who flourished during the Golden Age of Spain, there was no lovelier spirit than Judah Ha-Levi, the physician, philosopher, and above all, the greatest Hebrew poet between biblical and modern times.

Educated under the famed talmudist, Rabbi Isaac Alfasi, Judah mastered Hebrew as well as Arabic and Greek philosophy. He then studied medicine, but his passion was for poetry.

He poured out poems for festive occasions, wedding songs, riddles, and epigrams. As he matured, his poetry became more serious and moving. His words breathe the love of God and man. He expresses his longing for Zion and the hope that Palestine will one day belong again to the Jewish people.

Jewish suffering during the First Crusade and the weakening of faith made him rally to the defense of Judaism in the *Kuzari,* an account of the conversion to Judaism of Bulan, king of a faraway people called the Khazars.

Then, no longer content to sing of Zion, he yearned to make the pilgrimage to Palestine. When friends tried to discourage him, he said, "Shall a body of clay stop a soul urged on by eagle's wings?"

At the age of 55, he embarked on the perilous journey. He was wonderfully received wherever he stopped, but he would not be detained. His eyes were fixed on Jerusalem.

Whether he actually reached the City of David is shrouded in mystery. According to legend, he came at last to the Western Wall of the ancient Temple. As he kneeled to pray and sing his "Ode to Zion," a passing Arab horseman rode him down and killed him.

The "Ode to Zion" was the last poem he wrote. Eight centuries have passed, but it still fills us with sorrow and inspires us with hope. It is recited in synagogues on Tisha Be-Av, the day that commemorates the destruction of the Temple in Jerusalem.

Here are a few lines of his poem "Longing for Jerusalem," translated by Emma Lazarus:

O city of the world, with sacred splendor blest,
My spirit bends to thee from out the far-off West.
Had I an eagle's wing, straight would I fly to thee,
Moisten thy holy dust with wet cheeks streaming free.

24

POET OF PROPHECY

THE GOLDEN AGE OF SPAIN—10TH TO 13TH CENTURIES—MARKED A RICH FLOWERING OF JEWISH LITERATURE AND SCIENCE.

TOLEDO, IN 1085, SAW THE BIRTH OF JUDAH HA-LEVI, GREATEST HEBREW POET OF THE MIDDLE AGES.

AS A YOUTH, JUDAH STUDIED TALMUD, ARAB LITERATURE AND MEDICINE.

HE BECAME A PHYSICIAN, BUT HIS FIRST LOVE WAS HEBREW POETRY.

OH LORD, WHERE SHALL I FIND THEE? HIDDEN AND EXALTED IS THY PLACE...

A FELLOW-POET AND MUCH OLDER MAN, MOSES IBN-EZRA, SAID:

HOW CAN A BOY SO YOUNG BEAR SUCH A WEIGHT OF WISDOM?

AS HE GREW OLDER, HE LONGED TO SEE THE HOLY LAND.

MY HEART IS IN THE EAST BUT I AM IN THE WEST!

HOW THEN CAN I TASTE WHAT I EAT? HOW CAN FOOD TO ME BE SWEET?

HE DREAMT ONLY OF A ZION RESTORED TO OUR PEOPLE.

HIS FRIENDS WARNED HIM...

DON'T GO TO PALESTINE!

THE JOURNEY IS DANGEROUS!

MY SOUL IS URGED ON BY EAGLE'S WING!

IN 1140, HE SET OUT BY BOAT TO EGYPT, THEN TO TYRE, DAMASCUS, AND JERUSALEM...

LEGEND SAYS THAT AS HE APPROACHED THE WAILING WALL TO PRAY...

AN EVIL HORSEMAN SNUFFED OUT HIS LIFE.

HIS SONGS AND POEMS STILL INSPIRE US. HIS LYRICS ARE IN OUR PRAYER BOOK.

AND WE STILL REVERE THE NAME OF JUDAH HA-LEVI, OFTEN CALLED "THE SWEET SINGER OF ZION!"

MAIMONIDES

26

HIS name was Moses ben Maimon, or Maimonides, but he is also known simply as "the Rambam," from the initials of his name, *Rabbi Moses ben Maimon.*

Born in Cordova, Spain, on the eve of Passover, 1135, he grew up to be the greatest Jewish scholar of the Middle Ages. His genius showed itself in the study of Torah, philosophy, medicine, astronomy, and other subjects.

In 1148, Cordova fell to the Almohades, a war-loving sect of Moslems. The Maimon family wandered through Spain for ten years, sailing in 1159 for Fez, Morocco. The Almohades came to Morocco too, and in 1165, when Maimonides' teacher, Rabbi Judah ibn Shoshan, was killed, the family journeyed to Palestine.

The Holy Land was ruled by Crusaders who gave Jews little peace. The homeless Maimons sought refuge again, this time in Egypt. There they found freedom, and the Rambam settled down to study and write.

At 33, he completed the *Ma-or,* or "Light," a commentary on the Mishnah. Here he set down the "13 Principles of Faith" which became a guide to Judaism. The well-known hymn, *Yigdal,* still sung in the synagogue, is a poetic version of these principles.

When his dear brother David died, grief-stricken Maimonides was ill for a year. When he arose from his sickbed, he turned to the practice of medicine to keep his waking hours crowded with activity.

He kept at his studies too, and in 1180 completed the *Mishneh Torah,* a many-volumed work in which the Rambam collected all the laws of the Bible and Talmud, and those made later in Germany, France, and Spain. He also wrote the *Moreh Nevukhim* ("Guide for the Perplexed"), which tried to answer religious questions and problems, and the *Iggeret Teman* ("Letter to Yemen"), which encouraged his fellow Jews in Yemen to resist false leaders who were pressing them to desert the Jewish faith.

In the meantime, the Rambam's fame as a physician spread. He became the court doctor to the Sultan of Egypt. He also served as head of the Jewish community of Egypt, with the title of "Nagid."

He died in December, 1204. For three days, Moslems and Jews in Egypt mourned. In synagogues, a chapter was read from the Bible ending with the sentence, "The glory has departed from Israel, for the Ark of God is taken" (*I Samuel* 4:22). He was buried in Tiberias, Palestine, where his tomb is still visited by thousands.

Centuries ago, it was declared that the Rambam was one of the most remarkable men of all time. That judgment is still as true as ever.

'FROM MOSES TO MOSES'

BENJAMIN OF TUDELA

HAVE you ever heard of the Jewish merchant seamen of the Middle Ages? They charted new ocean routes and sent ships down the coast of Spain to Italy and North Africa.

These adventurers exchanged wares with lands as distant as China. They visited Mohammedan countries and brought back to Europe the first oranges and apricots, sugar and rice, cinnamon and slippers and sofas and jasmine. They also carried books and ideas, and sometimes even passengers. One of these travelers kept a lively diary in Hebrew, in which he recorded his experiences among fellow Jews in Southern Europe, Asia, and Africa.

Benjamin of Tudela started out from Saragossa, Spain, in 1160. In thirteen years he visited nearly 300 places in Provence, Italy, Greece, Cilicia, Palestine, Mesopotamia, Persia, and India. He returned by way of Aden, Yemen, Egypt, and Sicily.

He arrived in Rome about 1165 and came to Bagdad in 1168. He observed that the Jews of Bagdad were governed by Daniel the Exilarch, or Prince of the Exile, whose power extended over the Jews from Persia to Arabia and to Anatolia. All people honored him, and every Thursday the Exilarch went to pay his respects to the Mohammedan Caliph. Horsemen escorted him and heralds cried, *"I-milu tarik li Sayidna ibn Daoud!"* (Make way before our lord, the son of David.) At the time of Benjamin's visit, there were 40,000 Jews in Bagdad, and twenty-eight synagogues.

Benjamin observed the Mohammedan group called Assassins, who followed their chieftain with blind obedience. They would even murder to gain their ends. Their Arabic name was *hashashin,* from the *hashish* plant which they used as a drug.

Benjamin kept a list of the number of Jews living in each place he visited. He noted their occupations: silk weavers in Greece, dyers in Palestine, glassmakers and shipowners in Syria.

One of Benjamin's most remarkable experiences concerned a false Messiah who arose among the Jews of Persia. David Alroy declared that God had chosen him to deliver the Jews from Moslem rule and to lead them back to Jerusalem. David's claims proved worthless and he did much harm by raising false hopes.

Benjamin's diary, *The Travels of Rabbi Benjamin,* was published in Constantinople long after his death. The first English translation appeared in 1840; by then it had appeared in Latin and many other languages. Benjamin's *Travels* became a source book for historians. They found in it stories repeated by later travelers, including Marco Polo, who visited China twenty years after Benjamin.

We are indebted to Benjamin of Tudela, far-wandering traveler, for a fascinating account of a vanished world.

28

THE FAR-WANDERER

300 YEARS BEFORE COLUMBUS, IN THE 12th CENTURY, THERE LIVED IN SPAIN A MAN CALLED BENJAMIN. IN 1160...

WHERE TO NOW, BENJAMIN OF TUDELA?

I'M OFF TO VISIT MY FELLOW JEWS IN OTHER LANDS!

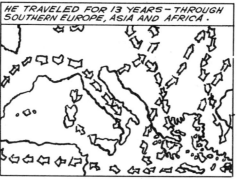

HE TRAVELED FOR 13 YEARS – THROUGH SOUTHERN EUROPE, ASIA AND AFRICA.

WHEN HE RETURNED IN 1173 HE WROTE OF HIS ADVENTURES IN A BOOK CALLED **TRAVELS OF RABBI BENJAMIN.**

HE WROTE MANY AN EXCITING TALE.

THE JEWS OF BAGDAD (HE WROTE) HAD A RULER KNOWN AS THE EXILARCH: **PRINCE OF THE EXILES.** HE WAS HONORED BY ALL MEN.

IT IS THURSDAY, YOUR EXCELLENCY.

AH! IT IS THE DAY TO VISIT THE MOHAMMEDAN RULER.

HERALDS PROCLAIMED HIS COMING.

MAKE WAY BEFORE OUR LORD, THE SON OF DAVID!

HE HAD A SPECIAL THRONE IN THE CALIPH'S PALACE, AND THE CALIPH HIM-SELF ROSE ...

PRAY BE SEATED, O EXILARCH!

BENJAMIN TOLD ABOUT THE JEWS IN PALESTINE...

"THEY ARE EXPERTS AT DYEING AND GLASS-MAKING..."

HE WROTE ABOUT THE BLACK JEWS OF MALABAR...

GREETING FROM THE WESTERN WORLD, MY FELLOW-JEWS!

HE TOLD OF A SEA STORM BETWEEN CEYLON AND CHINA.

THE SAILORS WRAPPED THEMSELVES IN CATTLE HIDES AND PLUNGED INTO THE OCEAN. GRIFFINS CARRIED THEM TO SHORE.

HE DESCRIBED A FALSE JEWISH LEADER IN PERSIA...

I AM DAVID ALROY, YOUR MESSIAH, SENT TO LEAD YOU TO EVERLASTING FREEDOM!

HE EVEN VISITED CHINA...

...AND SAW THE GREAT WALL, THEN OVER 1000 YEARS OLD.

HIS BOOK WAS TO BE TRANSLATED INTO MANY LANGUAGES, AND BENJAMIN WAS TO GO DOWN IN HISTORY AS THE FIRST MEDIEVAL TRAVELER EVER TO REACH THE ORIENT!

MEIR OF ROTHENBURG

RABBI MEIR BEN BARUCH was born in Germany between 1215 and 1220. People were often not very exact in those days about recording dates of birth. But his deeds were recorded in detail and they have come down to us as a shining example of dedication and selflessness.

Rabbi Meir served as a spiritual leader in a number of places, chiefly in Rothenburg, and he became so great an authority on Jewish law that he was known as the "Light of the Exile."

It was a time when the Exile itself was daily growing darker. With his own eyes, Rabbi Meir had seen twenty-four cartloads of Hebrew books thrown on the flames in Paris on a Sabbath eve. Persecution had overtaken the Jews in Germany as well. At the age of 66, Rabbi Meir was asked to lead a group of refugees who were determined to reach Palestine.

While waiting at Lombardy for the rest of his company to arrive he was recognized by a Jew who had left Judaism and was now accompanying the bishop of Basel. The bishop had Rabbi Meir seized and taken back to Germany. There, upon the order of Emperor Rudolf of Hapsburg, he was imprisoned in the fortress of Ensisheim.

Pidyon Shevu'im, the ransoming of captives, has always been among the most noble traditions of the Jewish people. The friends of Rabbi Meir offered the emperor 20,000 marks in silver for the release of their leader.

The rabbi, however, refused to be ransomed. He feared that if he permitted his friends to pay the money other rulers would kidnap rabbis in order to force their congregations to ransom them.

His students were permitted to meet with him and he was even able to compose several of his works within the prison walls. Rabbi Meir remained behind bars for seven years. At his death in 1293 the emperor once again demanded a heavy ransom before yielding the rabbi's body for burial.

It was years before the body was finally surrendered upon payment of a huge ransom by one Alexander Suskind Wimpfen who, in return, asked that after his own death his body should be laid to rest next to the saintly rabbi. His wish was carried out and in the Jewish cemetery of the city of Worms a double grave with a single tombstone marked the resting place of the rabbi and his loyal follower.

During his lifetime Rabbi Meir had kept up a talmudical academy at his own cost. His students brought his teachings to Austria, Spain, and Portugal.

As renowned as he was for his learning, however, it was his refusal to bring even the threat of sorrow to his people that enshrined his name in Jewish history.

30

THE PRISONER

NAHMANIDES

THE beginning of the end of the Golden Age in Spain is marked by the exile of one of the outstanding scholars and Bible commentators of the Middle Ages, Rabbi Moses ben Nahman, also called Nahmanides ("Son of Nahman"), also called Gerondi (he was born in Gerona, a city in Aragon, Spain), also called Ramban (from the initials of *R*abbi *M*oses *b*en *N*ahman).

Nahmanides lived quietly in Gerona, earning his living as a physician, studying and writing and growing in scholarship until he was widely acknowledged as the spiritual leader of Spanish Jewry.

Leadership carries with it responsibility, and fame is sometimes accompanied by misfortune.

Chief among the increasing number of enemies of the Jews were the Dominican friars, who were slyly suggesting to the king that there were too many Jews in high places. A favorite method of pointing an accusing finger was to challenge an intended victim to a religious debate. In these "disputations," Jews were called upon to defend their faith before the world.

When a Dominican friar named Pablo Christiani, who had once been a Jew himself, persuaded King James of Aragon to arrange a disputation with the most famous rabbi in Spain, there was only one man who could serve as defender.

In the year 1263, at the age of 68, Nahmanides reluctantly took up the challenge. The debate was held in the king's palace at Barcelona in the presence of nobility and churchmen. The judges were Christians. Nahmanides had but one slim hope: he had requested and received from King James permission for full freedom of speech.

Pablo began by reminding the judges that the Jews had always believed in a Messiah. He continued by describing Jesus as the true Messiah, and concluded by insisting that the Jews should accept Jesus as the Messiah and thus prove the greatness of Christianity.

Nahmanides replied with great strength and courage that the Jews did not believe that the Messiah would be a god. Furthermore, according to Jewish tradition, the Messiah's coming would bring peace, not bloodshed.

So successful was he that, after four days, his opponents were anxious to halt the debate, and the king dismissed Nahmanides with a gift of gold. The friars refused to admit defeat, however, and when Nahmanides published a true account of what had been said at the debate, they accused him of attacking their faith and had him banished from Aragon.

Nahmanides was 72 when he left his homeland. He came to Palestine, where he spent the remaining three years of his life rebuilding the scattered Jewish communities, giving public lectures, and completing his commentary on the Bible.

32

MAN OF MANY NAMES

THIS MAN HAD MANY NAMES...

HE WAS CALLED GERONDI (BECAUSE HE WAS BORN IN GERONA, SPAIN), AND HIS SPANISH NAME WAS... BONASTRUC DA PORTA.

BUT WE KNOW HIM AS NAHMANIDES OR THE RaMBaN, SHORT FOR RABBI MOSES BEN NAHMAN

BY DAY HE HEALED THE SICK ...

BY NIGHT HE STUDIED TORAH.

HE WROTE COMMENTARIES ON THE BIBLE AND TALMUD AND TAUGHT HIS PEOPLE.

THE SIX DAYS OF CREATION STAND FOR 6,000 YEARS THAT FOLLOW... AND THEN -- THE MESSIAH!

IN 1263, HIS QUIET LIFE SUDDENLY CHANGED.

KING JAMES I OF ARAGON SUMMONS YOU!

NAHMANIDES, THIS IS FRA PABLO, A JEW TURNED TRAITOR TO HIS FAITH. HE CHALLENGES YOUR PEOPLE TO A DEBATE ON RELIGION.

MAY I HAVE FULL FREEDOM OF SPEECH?

YES, I GUARANTEE IT!

AFTER 4 DAYS OF DEBATE...

NAHMANIDES, YOUR PRESENTATION HAS WON US ALL. YOU WIN THE DEBATE!

BRILLIANT!

WHAT AN ORATOR!

JEALOUS TONGUES BEGAN TO WAG...

HE'S AN ENEMY!

HE PLOTS AGAINST THE KING!

BANISH HIM, YOUR MAJESTY!

SADLY, THE RAMBAN LEFT HIS NATIVE LAND...

AND, AT 72 BEGAN LIFE ANEW IN PALESTINE, WHERE HE FOUND COMMUNITIES SCATTERED AND DESOLATE.

LET US RETURN TO JERUSALEM AND STUDY THE WORD OF GOD!

IN HAIFA, HE SPENT HIS LAST YEARS TEACHING AND WRITING. HIS NAME LIVES FOREVER, FOR HE WAS A HERO OF OUR PEOPLE.

ISAAC ABRAVANEL

THE Inquisition, first set up in 1248, gradually brought black night to the Golden Age of Jewry in Spain. Through special courts in charge of discovering and punishing those who offended Christianity, the Inquisition slowly destroyed the Jewish community. The final moment came when the monk Thomas de Torquemada influenced Queen Isabella and King Ferdinand to expel the Jews from Spain.

Among those who marched on that bitter day in 1492 was Don Isaac Abravanel. He had chosen to flee with his people rather than accept personal exemption.

Last of the great figures of the Golden Age, Isaac was born in 1437 to a family that traced its descent back to King David. Isaac followed his father, the state treasurer of Portugal, in the service of King Alfonso V. When the next king came to the throne, he accused Don Isaac of conspiracy, and Abravanel was forced to flee.

He arrived penniless in Toledo, Spain, with his wife and children, but his abilities in finance were soon recognized and he was made court treasurer in 1490. When the law expelling the Jews was announced, Don Isaac offered the king 30,000 gold ducats in the hope that the decree would be repealed.

Abravanel's talents were extremely useful, and he was offered the right to remain. But he refused, and when his gift was rejected, Don Isaac joined the cavalcade of refugees.

His next stop was in Naples, where he was called into the king's service. Naples, however, was captured by Charles of France in 1495, and once more Abravanel and his family had to escape.

He wandered from Naples to the island of Corfu in the Mediterranean; from there to North Africa; from there to Venice, where he found peace in 1503. It was not long before the Doge of Venice invited Abravanel to journey to Lisbon and arrange a commercial treaty between Portugal and the Venetian Republic.

During these troubled and difficult years, he somehow managed to write commentaries on the Bible which were so popular that no less than thirty Christian scholars made translations of them. He also wrote forward-looking political works, in which he favored rulers who were elected for a limited time.

The autobiographical notes which he left at his death in Venice in 1508 are very revealing. There is not a word in them of complaint about his sufferings or loss of fortune; not a note of boasting concerning his triumphal return, as an ambassador of a foreign power, to Lisbon, from which he had once been driven.

He died as he had lived, a nobleman in manner, mind, and soul.

34

THE NOBLE REFUGEE

FRIENDS OF COLUMBUS

36

WAS Columbus a Jew? No one knows for certain, although according to one fascinating theory, he was born in Spain to Jewish parents and he hid the secret of his Jewish origin behind a Marrano's mask.

Columbus himself wrote, in one of his letters: "I am not the first Admiral of my family; for David was first a shepherd and afterwards King of Jerusalem, and I am a servant of that same Lord Who raised him to such dignity." And in his will Columbus directed that a "half-mark of silver be paid to a Jew dwelling at the gate of the Jewish section of Lisbon."

However, while scholars still debate the Jewish origin of the man who set sail on his historic voyage on August 3, 1492, everyone agrees that the aid of Jews in the success of Columbus' project was of the highest importance.

In Portugal he studied the charts of Judah Cresques, known as the "map-Jew." At the Portuguese court he met the royal physician, Joseph Vecinho, who had translated into Spanish the astronomical tables written in Hebrew by Abraham Zacuto. Columbus carried these charts with him on his voyages.

His closest Jewish friends were two Marranos at the Spanish court. They were Luis de Santangel, chancellor of the royal household, and Gabriel Sanchez, chief treasurer of Aragon.

Columbus had asked for the title of Admiral and a share in all the profits of any new lands he might discover. Turned down by the throne, he was on his way to plead his case at the court of France when he was overtaken by a messenger.

Queen Isabella had agreed to his demands. Santangel had pleaded for him and had offered to pay half the cost of the voyage. Columbus later showed his gratitude by sending his first letter from the New World to Luis de Santangel.

Columbus' second voyage in 1493 was paid for by the wealth taken away from Jews expelled the year before, from silk and velvet Torah mantles, and gold and silver ceremonial objects. A historian has said, "Not jewels, but Jews" paid for Columbus' expeditions.

The crew of the first voyage included a number of Jews. Luis de Torres, who understood Hebrew, Chaldaic, and Arabic, was the interpreter; Roderigo Sanchez was related to the royal treasurer; Maestre Bernal and Dr. Marco were the ships' surgeons; and there was one Alonso de la Calle, a former resident of Jews' Lane, for which he was named.

In the year of their bitter exile from the land which had provided a Golden Age for our people, Jews helped discover a new land which was to be a haven of refuge and freedom in modern times.

THE NEW WORLD

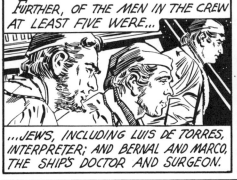

DANIEL BOMBERG

AN amazing man, Daniel Bomberg. He was a Flemish Christian aristocrat who became an important printer and publisher of Hebrew books. Born in Antwerp in the 1480's, he died in Venice in 1549.

He helped create the Hebrew printed book, for it was in the mid-15th century that printing from movable type was invented in Europe, and it was in 1475 that the first Jewish book, an edition of Rashi's commentary on the Bible, came off the press.

Before that time, books were copied by scribes, who would often illustrate them artistically and in many colors. Since the rabbis forbade any illustration of the Torah, scribes would save some of their richest drawings for the Passover Haggadah. This practice has lived on to this very day, and many Haggadahs now in use are full of beautiful illustrations.

Printing changed the form of the Jewish book for all time. From Italy, the art of Hebrew printing spread to Spain and Portugal. After Jews were driven from Spain in 1492, the art moved, along with Spanish Jews, to all the countries of the world in which they settled.

But back to Daniel Bomberg. At the beginning of the 16th century, he settled in Venice, where he established his press. He employed Jewish assistants and had many learned men on his staff.

With their help he obtained valuable manuscripts of the Bible and of the Talmud, and together they tried to establish accurate texts. One authority said of Bomberg: "He studied Hebrew and crowned himself therewith."

The first great work published by Bomberg's press was the complete text of the Bible in Hebrew with many old and new commentaries.

With the permission of Pope Leo X, Bomberg issued the first complete edition of the Babylonian Talmud. It set the style for all editions ever printed thereafter.

He printed many other Hebrew books. When he grew old, he turned his press over to his son David. Upon the death of Daniel Bomberg, David became the owner of the famous Bomberg press which, before the 17th century, issued more Hebrew books than any other press.

Unfortunately, Daniel Bomberg paid dearly for his fame. The excellence of his work attracted imitators who became wealthy. But Bomberg himself spent so much money on paper and engravings that before his death he had lost almost his whole fortune.

Bomberg's work had a powerful effect on Jewish life. Although books were still scarce, there were more of them than before. They came down in price and, before long, there was a copy of the Bible not only in the dwellings of the rich, but in every Jewish home.

There is a saying about the Jewish people and the Torah. "Jews have preserved the Book, and the Book has preserved Jewry."

Men like Daniel Bomberg did much to make that statement true.

38

THE MASTER PRINTER

TO THE JEW OF THE LATE MIDDLE AGES, VENICE WAS THE CITY OF BOOKS.

IN THE EARLY 1500'S, BEFORE THE VENETIAN SENATE.

I AM DANIEL BOMBERG, NEWLY ARRIVED FROM ANTWERP. I REQUEST PERMISSION TO PRINT HEBREW BOOKS.

YOU ARE A CHRISTIAN. WHY THIS REQUEST?

THE SACRED HEBREW BOOKS MUST NOT PERISH. WE CAN ALL LEARN FROM THEM.

HE RECEIVED PERMISSION.

AH! NOW I MUST GET SCHOLARS OF THE FIRST RANK!

BOMBERG SELECTED A STAFF: ELIJAH LEVITA, THE GRAMMARIAN; JACOB BEN HAYYIM...

...AND HIYYA MEIR, RABBI OF VENICE. TOGETHER WE WILL DO WONDERS!

BOMBERG OBTAINED SPECIAL RIGHTS FOR HIS STAFF.

NO ONE WORKING HERE NEED WEAR THE JEWISH HAT OF DISCRIMINATION IN VENICE!

RABBI HIYYA, FIRST I WILL LEARN HEBREW MYSELF

GOOD! LET US BEGIN WITH GENESIS.

ON NOV. 30, 1516, BOMBERG PUBLISHED THE FIRST PRODUCT OF HIS PRESS.

GENTLEMEN— THE TORAH— THE FIVE BOOKS OF MOSES!

ALL PRAISE TO YOU, DANIEL!

IN 1518, BOMBERG SAW POPE LEO X.

I GRANT YOU PERMISSION TO PUBLISH THE TALMUD IN VENICE!

MY EVERLASTING THANKS, YOUR EMINENCE!

ON JUNE 3, 1523, THE TREMENDOUS UNDERTAKING WAS COMPLETED.

THE WHOLE TALMUD!

THE FIRST COMPLETE EDITION IN HISTORY!

TO THIS DAY, AFTER 400 YEARS, THE TALMUD IS STILL PRINTED IN THE MANNER SET BY BOMBERG.

HE DIED IN 1549; HIS SON CARRIED ON.

JEWISH SCHOLARSHIP OWES AN EVER-LASTING DEBT TO DANIEL BOMBERG, MASTER PRINTER!

JOSEPH NASI

WHEN the Church forced the Jews of Portugal to become Christians in the late 1490's, many of them continued to practice Judaism secretly. These secret Jews were called Marranos, which is Spanish for "pigs."

The Mendez family of Lisbon were Marrano bankers with branch offices in Holland and business connections with the rulers of France. They had long hoped to move to a land where they might cease to be Marranos. When Francisco Mendez, the head of the family, died in 1536, his widow, Beatrice de Luna, left for Antwerp. She took along her daughter Reyna, her nephew Joao Miguez, and other relatives.

Prominent and envied in Antwerp because of her great wealth and charm, Beatrice Mendez soon was faced with additional danger. She had refused to give her daughter's hand in marriage to a number of young noblemen. Tongues wagged: how could she be a truly loyal Christian? Also, Joao Miguez, dashing and clever, was attracting attention and jealousy at the court.

Dona Beatrice and her family fled to Venice. But Venice was a Christian state and very often was used by Marranos on their way to Turkey. Beatrice was arrested for deserting Christianity and her property was seized by the government.

It is often darkest before dawn. Joao Miguez escaped to Turkey, where the sultan, dazzled by the prospect of having the Mendez fortune in his country, declared that Dona Beatrice was under his protection. The words of this powerful ruler were not to be ignored, and Venice released Beatrice Mendez and her wealth.

Once in Moslem Turkey, the family was at last able to shed its Marrano cloak and live openly as Jews. Beatrice changed her name to Gracia. Joao proudly adopted his Jewish name, Joseph Nasi, and married his cousin Reyna.

Joseph Nasi became the favorite of the sultan, and was rewarded by the sultan's son, when he succeeded his father, by being made Duke of the Island of Naxos in the Aegean Sea. He was also given the city of Tiberias in Palestine.

Here he attempted to build a Jewish colony. He planted mulberry trees for silkworm culture, and arranged for ships to bring refugees from Europe. Unfortunately, his plan to establish a Jewish homeland failed, for war broke out between Venice and Turkey, and Joseph had to fight for his position at the sultan's court.

Torn between the desire to redeem Palestine and the need to maintain his personal power, Joseph Nasi accomplished neither. His deeds did not endure beyond his death in 1579, but his story still holds the imagination, for he was a vigorous symbol of Jewish striving for emancipation.

40

THE DUKE OF NAXOS

AT 15, JOSEPH WAS A REFUGEE. WHEN HE DIED, HE WAS ONE OF THE MOST INFLUENTIAL MEN IN EUROPE.. ANTWERP, 16th CENTURY.

YOU HAVE EVERYTHING, JOSEPH. WHY ARE YOU SO UNHAPPY?

AUNT GRACIA, I CANNOT GO ON PRETENDING I AM A NON-JEW. LET US LEAVE FOR TURKEY.

IN VENICE, GRACIA WAS IMPRISONED FOR FOLLOWING THE JEWISH FAITH.

TO SULEIMAN II, SULTAN OF TURKEY! HELP RELEASE MY AUNT AND I WILL BRING MY WEALTH TO YOUR LAND! --- JOSEPH NASI.

THE SULTAN SENT AN AMBASSADOR.

GO TO VENICE. OBTAIN DONA GRACIA'S RELEASE. BRING HER AND JOSEPH HERE TO CONSTANTINOPLE!

HERE WE CAN OBSERVE OUR FAITH! HERE WE WILL BREATHE FREE!

ONE DAY - THERE IS A CALLER, SIRE. HIS NAME IS SELIM.

ELDEST SON OF THE SULTAN! SHOW HIM IN!

YOU HAVE BEEN MY FATHER'S FAVORITE, JOSEPH, AND YOUR NAME IS A GOOD ONE. MY FATHER IS DYING. WILL YOU SUPPORT MY RIGHTFUL CLAIM TO THE THRONE AGAINST MY BROTHER?

WHEN SELIM BECAME SULTAN ....

FOR SERVICE TO THE SULTAN, DON JOSEPH NASI IS MADE DUKE OF THE ISLAND OF NAXOS AND AWARDED THE CITY OF TIBERIAS IN PALESTINE!

THE DUKE OF NAXOS WAS PROUD OF HIS JEWISH HERITAGE ....

HE FOUNDED A JEWISH SCHOOL OF STUDY IN CONSTANTINOPLE ....

HE FOUNDED A HEBREW PRINTING PRESS.

AND INVITED REFUGEES TO SETTLE IN TIBERIAS. WE WILL PLANT MULBERRY TREES FOR SILKWORM CULTURE, AND WE WILL MANUFACTURE FINE WOOLENS.

NOT ALL HIS PLANS SUCCEEDED. BUT JOSEPH NASI, ADVENTURER AND STATESMAN, BECAME A SYMBOL OF JEWISH HOPES AND STRIVINGS FOR FREEDOM AND THE RE-BIRTH OF ISRAEL!

SHABBATAI ZEVI

TWO tremendous events took place in 1648. One was the Cossack uprising against Polish rule, led by a ruthless man named Chmielnicki. In the course of this struggle, about 300,000 Ukrainian Jews were massacred.

Depressed and exhausted, the survivors felt that the end of the world was at hand, for it was an old tradition that when the suffering of the Jewish people reached its most desperate point, God would send the Messiah to save them.

Now for the second event. During that same year of 1648, a young Turkish Jew proclaimed to the world that he was the true Messiah.

Shabbatai Zevi had been born in Smyrna, Turkey, in 1626. Attracted to the study of the mystic books of the Cabbalah, he drew from them the theory that the Messiah was due to arrive in 1648. He fasted, he prayed, he bathed in the sea on icy winter days. In 1648 he revealed to his disciples that he was the Messiah, destined by God to redeem Israel.

The Jewish community of Smyrna was horrified and threw him out of the city. He began his wanderings, and journeyed to Salonika, to Cairo, and to Jerusalem.

In Cairo, he heard of a lovely Jewish maiden named Sarah who believed she was destined to be the bride of the Messiah. Sarah was sent for, and Shabbatai married her amid great festivity.

His reputation spread everywhere and he was soon so renowned that he dared return to his native city. In 1665, to the blowing of trumpets, he entered the Smyrna synagogue and declared that he was the anointed Messiah. People were overwhelmed and prepared to follow him to Palestine.

They sold their possessions and bought food in readiness for the trip to Palestine. They refused to call doctors for the sick, uttering instead the name of Shabbatai Zevi in the hope that it would heal them.

In 1666, he set sail for Constantinople, Turkey. The sultan had heard that Shabbatai wished to take Palestine from him and give it to the Jews. Shabbatai expected a royal reception. Instead, on landing, he was thrown into prison. The sultan sentenced him to death and said that the only way Shabbatai Zevi could save his life was to become a Moslem.

Standing before the sultan, Shabbatai lost his courage and put on a white turban as a sign that he accepted Islam. The "Messiah" was nothing but a fraud!

Jews the world over were stunned. Why was the man who had promised to redeem Israel so ready to give up his faith? An empire of hopes and dreams had been cruelly shattered.

Shabbatai was banished by the sultan to Dulcino, a small Albanian town, where he lived until the age of 50. There he died on Yom Kippur of 1676. Other imposters took his place, but none ever had the magnetic attraction of Shabbatai Zevi.

42

THE FALSE MESSIAH

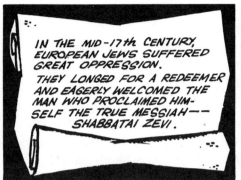

MANASSEH BEN ISRAEL

JEWISH settlement in England began in the 11th century, when William the Conqueror crossed from France to establish Norman rule over Great Britain. Jews paid heavy taxes to the royal treasury and were protected by the king when it was in his interest to do so. By the end of the 13th century, impoverished and persecuted, they were no longer useful to the throne and, on November 30, 1290, the entire community of 16,000 souls was forced to take the lonely road of exile.

For the next 350 years there was no Jewish community in England. There were some Portuguese Marranos, but they did not live openly as Jews. Then a combination of circumstances and the mystic views of a Sephardic Jew helped open the gates of England.

In the 16th century, England broke with the Catholic Church. At the same time, in nearby Holland, Jews who had escaped from the Inquisition had enriched the economy of the Netherlands. In 1642 the Bible-loving Puritans rebelled against the British throne. These facts helped set the stage. Now someone was needed to play the leading role.

That someone was Manasseh ben Israel, a Lisbon-born rabbi who, at 18, was appointed spiritual leader of Neveh Shalom Congregation in Amsterdam. A man of many interests, he became a printer and published his own works.

One of his books was *The Hope of Israel,* in which he developed the strange theory that the American Indians were the Ten Lost Tribes of Israel. Learned Christians hailed Manasseh's notion. Many believed that the Messiah would come only after the Jews had been widely scattered. Since England seemed to be the only place where there were no Jews, Manasseh was encouraged to discuss the matter with Britain's Lord Protector, Oliver Cromwell.

Manasseh arrived in London in 1655 and presented a petition to Cromwell, who proceeded to convene a conference at Whitehall to debate the issue. There was a flood of talk. Lawyers said that no new law was necessary to re-admit Jews, but no agreement on their return could be reached. Ashamed and irritated, Cromwell dismissed the Whitehall Conference. Manasseh lingered in London for a time, but finally returned to Holland, tired and disappointed. He died shortly thereafter, in November of 1657.

Though he considered himself a failure, he had succeeded far beyond his hopes. Since it had been established that there was no legal opposition, Marranos began to live more openly and, little by little, small groups of Jews began to enter England. Before many years had passed, there was a synagogue in London, and a Jewish community in the British Isles had been born.

44

HE OPENED THE GATES

IN THE YEAR 1290, KING EDWARD I PROCLAIMED: "ALL JEWS MUST LEAVE ENGLAND!"

FOR 350 YEARS, ONLY SMALL GROUPS OF MARRANOS (SECRET JEWS) MANAGED TO LIVE IN GREAT BRITAIN.

THEN AROSE A RABBI IN AMSTERDAM, HOLLAND.

IF WE ARE SOMEDAY TO RETURN TO ISRAEL, WE MUST FIRST BE SCATTERED IN ALL OTHER LANDS, IN ENGLAND....

BUT ENGLAND IS CLOSED TO JEWS!

HER GATES MUST BE OPENED! I WILL APPEAL TO OLIVER CROMWELL, LORD PROTECTOR OF ENGLAND!

ON SEPTEMBER 2, 1655, MANASSEH BEN ISRAEL SET OUT ON HIS MISSION WITH HIS SON SAMUEL.

CROMWELL IS A PURITAN. HE MUST BELIEVE WE ARE THE PEOPLE OF THE BIBLE. I WILL PREPARE A PETITION.

MANASSEH SAW OLIVER CROMWELL.

LORD PROTECTOR, WE WILL BENEFIT YOUR COUNTRY, AS WE HAVE AMSTERDAM, LEGHORN, NICE...

THE COUNCIL OF STATE WILL CONSIDER YOUR PLEA, RABBI.

MANASSEH SPENT HIS NIGHTS WRITING PAMPHLETS

"OUR NATION, NOW SCATTERED"

"...FAVOR AND GOOD WILL..."

"THE HOPE OF ISRAEL..."

SOME ENGLISH MERCHANTS FEARED COMPETITION. THIS ANGERED CROMWELL.

HOW CAN YOU-NOBLE MERCHANTS ALL-BE AFRAID OF PEOPLE YOU CONSIDER "INFERIOR"?

THE GOVERNMENT REFUSED TO ISSUE A FORMAL DECLARATION. CRUSHED, RABBI MANASSEH WENT HOME.

I HAVE BEEN A FAILURE.

HE DIED - ON NOVEMBER 20, 1657. THESE WORDS ARE ON HIS TOMBSTONE:

MANASSEH ben ISRAEL

HE IS NOT DEAD - IN HEAVEN HE LIVES, WHILE ON EARTH HIS PEN HAS WON HIM ETERNAL REMEMBRANCE.

IN 1660, CHARLES II ASCENDED THE THRONE OF ENGLAND. HE WAS A MERRY, TOLERANT MONARCH.

HAIL! HAIL!

FATHER OF OUR PEOPLE!

HAIL, KING CHARLES!

IN 1664, RESETTLEMENT OF JEWS IN ENGLAND WAS ASSURED BY A CHARTER. MANASSEH'S PEN HAD INDEED WON HIM "ETERNAL REMEMBRANCE."

ASSER LEVY

IN September, 1654, the French vessel *St. Charles* sailed slowly into New Amsterdam carrying twenty-three "healthy but poor" men, women, and children. They were to become the first Jewish community to settle in what is now the United States.

The twenty-three had set out from Recife, Brazil, in January, 1654, when the town was captured from the Dutch by the Portuguese, who ordered all Dutch subjects to leave. A vessel carrying the twenty-three was attacked by pirates who looted the ship. Rescued by the *St. Charles,* the refugees were set ashore penniless in New Amsterdam.

They were met by the only Jewish settler in New Amsterdam, Jacob Barsimson, who had come from Holland a month earlier.

With their arrival, the Jews' troubles increased. Peter Stuyvesant, the governor general of the colony and a supporter of the Dutch Reformed Church, had little use for any of the other religious groups in the colony—Huguenots, Moravians, Presbyterians, or Jews—but it was the Jews whom he disliked especially.

However, the Dutch West India Company, which had established the colony, told Stuyvesant not to disturb the Jews. Encouraged, the group sought to share the duties of the community. Asser Levy petitioned for the right to stand guard in the town as other burghers did. Until then, Jews had been taxed instead. Levy

won and thus became the first Jewish soldier in North America.

He then petitioned for burgher rights, which, when granted, gave him his citizenship.

The colony's major industry in those days was fur trading with the Indians, and Levy, after opposition from business rivals, succeeded in establishing the right of free trade throughout the colony.

Levy became one of the six licensed butchers in the community, but because of his religion, was excused from slaughtering hogs.

While the little band of Jews was winning these rights, similar groups were carrying on the same fight elsewhere. In 1655 Jews came to Delaware, in 1656 to Maryland, in 1658 to Newport, Rhode Island, and in later years to Philadelphia, Charleston, and other towns.

After the United States was established, Jewish immigration, like that of other groups, came in waves. In the nineteenth century, Jews came from Germany, Holland, and England. Oppression of Jews in Poland and Russia encouraged immigration from Eastern Europe. The next large-scale move was spurred by Hitler's cruelties.

Historically, Asser Levy helped found the tradition of religious liberty in the New World. He set a pattern for future Jewish immigrants, all of whom gave something to America in return for its freedoms and protections.

THE FIRST CITIZEN

THE BA'AL SHEM TOV

TWO and a half centuries ago Polish Jews led an unhappy life. Lonely and scattered, they had suffered much persecution.

At that time there came into the world a great man who was to bring joy to his people. Israel, the son of Eliezer, was born in 1700. Later he became known as the Ba'al Shem Tov ("master of the good name") or *Besht,* an abbreviation formed from the first letters of his title.

48

His parents died when he was still a little child, and the good people of his village took care of the orphan and sent him to the *heder.* But Israel was different from the other children. He loved nature and would often leave his lessons to wander in the nearby woods.

At 20, Israel married, and he and his wife made their home in a town at the foot of the Carpathian Mountains, where the Besht wandered among the poor peasants and learned to use plants and herbs to make simple medicines.

His thoughts were always of the Creator. He saw God everywhere and felt His presence in everything. He told the poor of his people that if they served God with joy, their lives would be joyous. Sadness and weeping, he said, hurt the soul of a man.

The Besht traveled from town to town and the people loved him, for he shared their sorrow and brought light into dreary lives. Followers flocked to him and

thus began the movement known as *Hassidism,* for his disciples were the "Hassidim"—the pious.

The Besht came to a wounded people. In the terrible Chmielnicki massacres 600,000 Jews had been murdered and over 700 communities wiped out. Bewildered people hungered for a plain and simple faith which they could understand and follow.

He had a way of teaching which was clear and he illustrated his lessons with little stories. He said that the most important thing was to believe and trust in God. Second in importance was the joy of prayer, which was greater than learning, for prayer brought man close to God. Even a simple woodsman or farmer could reach God with a heartfelt prayer.

The Besht loved Jews, all of them together and each one individually. He would allow no harsh word to be uttered about anyone. All men are dear to God, he said.

The Hassidic movement spread quickly through the Ukraine, Poland, Galicia, Lithuania—in fact, throughout Eastern Europe. The Besht died in 1760. His disciples became the leaders of Hassidism and thousands came to them to benefit from their wisdom and learning.

Hassidism was a vital Jewish movement created by a magnetic Jewish personality whose teachings still live in the world of Jewish thought.

THE BOY WHO WHISTLED

SOLOMON DA COSTA

THE history books tell us very little about the imaginative and generous Solomon da Costa.

They reveal only that he collected Hebrew books, that he was a broker by profession, and that he gathered a large fortune, much of which he distributed as charity to non-Jews as well as to Jews.

But he is especially worth honoring because through him was preserved the division of Hebrew books in the library of London's British Museum. These had been brought together during the period of the Commonwealth, from 1642 to 1660, when no one sat on England's throne.

When the monarchy was restored in Great Britain in 1660, the books came into the royal possession of England's new king, Charles II. This fun-loving monarch had no interest in such matters as Hebrew books and he paid scant attention to them. Nor did the following rulers, James II and William III.

At last, in the reign of Queen Anne, they were sold to a bookseller, from whom, some time later, the entire collection was purchased by Solomon da Costa. The library which he presented to the British Museum grew into 40,000 Hebrew books and manuscripts which are today part of the huge "Department of Oriental Printed Books and Manuscripts." These precious materials are studied and used by many scholars. Photographs of manuscripts are made for those who wish to pore over them in other lands.

The British Museum has been a house of study to many persons in the more than 200 years of its existence. About 300 persons of various ages and races bend over books and scribble notes at any time of the day in its Reading Room. Over six million books line its encircling stacks.

It offers to the public exhibits of rare objects. One of the most famous of its exhibits is the Rosetta Stone, a war prize of Admiral Nelson's expedition against Napoleon's forces in Egypt. It was a Frenchman, Jean François Champollion, who won the greatest glory from the Rosetta Stone by using it to decipher Egyptian hieroglyphics.

Another great archeological treasure are the Elgin marbles, taken from a frieze of the Parthenon in the days when rich Englishmen scoured the Eastern Mediterranean for antiquities.

It is to this noble institution that Solomon da Costa made his presentation in the middle of the 18th century. There are other Jewish departments in general libraries and there are Jewish libraries. Some have more Jewish books than has the British Museum, but no Jewish book collection had so special and romantic a beginning as did that of the British Museum, which grew from a seed sown by a man with a far-seeing plan.

50

THE SEED THAT GREW

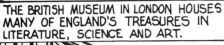

THE BRITISH MUSEUM IN LONDON HOUSES MANY OF ENGLAND'S TREASURES IN LITERATURE, SCIENCE AND ART.

ITS DEPARTMENT OF ORIENTAL BOOKS AND MANUSCRIPTS HAS THOUSANDS OF JEWISH BOOKS AND MANUSCRIPTS.

BUT WHEN THE BRITISH MUSEUM WAS FOUNDED IN 1753, ITS HEBRAIC SECTION HAD...

... ONE JEWISH VOLUME.

A FEW YEARS LATER, AN IMMIGRANT JEW FROM HOLLAND CAME TO KING GEORGE II.

YOUR MAJESTY, I AM SOLOMON DA COSTA, MERCHANT, NOTARY, SCRIBE, AND... A MAN WITH A REQUEST.

STATE YOUR REQUEST.

I SHOULD LIKE TO PURCHASE THE HOLY HEBREW BOOKS OWNED BY A LOCAL BOOKSELLER.

WHY DO YOU REQUIRE THE CROWN'S PERMISSION?

AH, SUCH VOLUMES! A TORAH ON PARCHMENT WITH POINTS AND ACCENTS, WRITINGS OF MAIMONIDES, OF RASHI, OF JOSEPH CARO! OLD BOOKS! PRICELESS BOOKS!

BUT WHY OUR PERMISSION?

YOUR MAJESTY, THESE 200 VOLUMES ONCE BELONGED TO KING CHARLES II. HE LOST THEM, ALAS, BY NOT PAYING A BOOKBINDER'S BILL.

I SEE! YOU'VE FOUND THEM AND YOU DON'T WANT THE KING TO CLAIM THEM LATER. YOU'LL SELL THEM DEARLY!

NO, YOUR MAJESTY! I WANT TO **GIVE THEM** AWAY!

THESE ARE TREASURES OF MY PEOPLE. I WILL OFFER THEM TO THE NEW BRITISH MUSEUM. PERHAPS, LIKE A PLANTED SEED, THE COLLECTION WILL GROW!

A SPLENDID IDEA. WE RELEASE ALL CLAIMS... TO SOLOMON DA COSTA, MERCHANT, SCRIBE, AND...NOBLE SOUL!

DA COSTA BOUGHT THE PRECIOUS VOLUMES, CATALOGUED THEM IN HEBREW, LATIN, AND ENGLISH...

... AND PRESENTED THEM TO THE BRITISH MUSEUM!

THE WORLD-FAMOUS COLLECTION NOW NUMBERS 40,000 BOOKS AND MANUSCRIPTS, FRUIT OF THE SEED PLANTED BY— SOLOMON DA COSTA!

MOSES MENDELSSOHN

MOSES MENDELSSOHN was a man with a mission: he wanted to break down the ghetto walls that hemmed in German Jewry.

Born in Dessau, Germany, to Mendel the *Sofer* (Torah scribe), Moses was educated by the local rabbi, David Hirschel Frankel, whom he followed to Berlin in 1743 at the age of 14. He then began to study mathematics, Latin, Greek, and philosophy, while he continued his Jewish studies, concentrating on the works of Maimonides.

He met important people in the world of literature and art and his home became a meeting place for many of the outstanding thinkers of the day. Mendelssohn was witty, intelligent, and a sparkling conversationalist. It was said that French noblemen, on visiting Germany, declared that they had come only to see the king and Mendelssohn. You must bear in mind that this was a time when German Jews still had to live in ghettos and special permission was necessary for a Jew to live in Berlin.

Mendelssohn was very active in Jewish affairs. The best-known Jew in Germany, he used his influence to help Jewish communities in his own country and elsewhere. He felt that the way to destroy ghetto walls was to bring the outside world to his people and to lead his people to the world beyond the ghetto.

Mendelssohn opened a free school in Berlin where Jewish boys were trained in trades and were taught the German language as well as Bible and Talmud. He translated the Five Books of Moses and *Psalms* into German, and published the German translation, in Hebrew letters, next to the Hebrew text. From this translation many Talmud students learned the German language and went on to study general subjects.

Mendelssohn wrote *Jerusalem,* in which he showed that a Jew could be loyal to religious tradition and yet be modern in outlook. He asked for equality for all citizens without regard to creed.

While pleading for tolerance, Mendelssohn cautioned his fellow-Jews to keep up their Jewish traditions and ceremonial laws. He had been so successful in battering down the ghetto walls, however, that for some this warning came too late. Among his followers were those who were so eager to grasp the cultural and economic opportunities offered them that they broke completely with Judaism. They hoped that by doing this, Jews would be more readily accepted by their non-Jewish neighbors. Mendelssohn's own daughters embraced Christianity.

Mendelssohn's place in Jewish history is very secure. He built a road from the ghetto to the world outside. He did not intend it to become, as it did for some, a one-way street.

52

HE BROKE THE GHETTO WALLS

THE YEAR: 1743. THE PLACE: THE JEWS' GATE OF BERLIN.

LOOK BOY, NO JEW MAY LIVE HERE UNLESS HE'S WEALTHY, OR A RABBI, OR A DOCTOR. WHOM DO YOU KNOW HERE?

RABBI DAVID FRANKEL. I'VE COME TO STUDY WITH HIM.

THE GATEKEEPER TOOK PITY. AT RABBI FRANKEL'S HOUSE...

WELL, MOSES MENDELSSOHN, YOU'RE HERE. WHY HAVE YOU COME?

TO STUDY. THERE'S NO ONE IN DESSAU TO TEACH ME.

FOR 7 YEARS, MOSES LIVED IN AN ATTIC.

I MUST STUDY EVERYTHING: BIBLE, AND TALMUD, AND — YES — LATIN, FRENCH, GERMAN AND PHILOSOPHY.

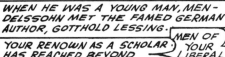

WHEN HE WAS A YOUNG MAN, MENDELSSOHN MET THE FAMED GERMAN AUTHOR, GOTTHOLD LESSING.

YOUR RENOWN AS A SCHOLAR HAS REACHED BEYOND THE GHETTO. WE CHRISTIANS RESPECT YOU, MENDELSSOHN.

MEN OF YOUR LIBERAL SPIRIT ARE HELPING US BREAK GHETTO WALLS!

YEARS LATER, LESSING WROTE A PLAY.

WHAT'S THE PLAY ABOUT?

IT'S SAID THAT LESSING USED MOSES MENDELSSOHN AS A MODEL FOR NATHAN!

by Gottwald LESSING

ON THE STAGE, NATHAN THE WISE SAID:

JEWS, CHRISTIANS, MOHAMMEDANS, ARE LIKE BROTHERS, AS LONG AS THEY ACT HONESTLY AND KINDLY.

BRAVO!

BRAVO!

BRAVO!

IT WAS STARTLING IN THOSE DAYS TO HEAR THAT JEWS WERE AS GOOD AS CHRISTIANS.

IN 1761, MOSES MARRIED FROMET GUGGENHEIM.

SEE MY HUNCHED BACK, FROMET? IN HEAVEN I HEARD IT DECREED THAT FROMET WAS TO BE BORN THUS, BUT I INSISTED ON HAVING IT SO THAT YOU MIGHT BE STRAIGHT AND BEAUTIFUL!

YOU ARE A POET, MOSES.

TO HELP HIS CHILDREN LEARN THE BIBLE, MOSES UNDERTOOK A HUGE PROJECT.

I WILL TRANSLATE THE 5 BOOKS OF MOSES INTO GERMAN WITH A HEBREW COMMENTARY.

THUS MY CHILDREN WILL STUDY THE BIBLE AND LEARN GERMAN AT THE SAME TIME.

IN 5 YEARS, THE TASK WAS DONE. IT WON HIM BOTH FRIENDS AND ENEMIES.

WHAT A DEVILISH THING TO DO!

WONDERFUL! IT OPENS UP THE WORLD FOR US!

HE SPOKE FOR OUR PEOPLE. HE OPPOSED UNFAIR TAXES AND HELPED FOUND THE FIRST TRULY MODERN JEWISH SCHOOL IN BERLIN.

HERE WE WILL STUDY LANGUAGES AND SCIENCE AS WELL AS JEWISH SUBJECTS.

HE DIED IN 1786, AND OTHERS CARRIED ON HIS WORK. A CENTURY LATER, THE CITY OF DESSAU ERECTED A MONUMENT TO HONOR MOSES MENDELSSOHN, WHO HELPED BREAK DOWN GHETTO WALLS.

LEVI YITZHAK OF BERDITCHEV

HE loved God and he loved the common man. That sums up the warm and tender personality of Rabbi Levi Yitzhak of Berditchev.

He lived and breathed Hassidism almost from the moment he was born in 1740, for he came from a long line of rabbis, and his teacher was Rabbi Dov Ber of Meseritz, disciple of the Ba'al Shem Tov. For his bride he chose the daughter of Shneur Zalman of Ladi, founder of the Habad branch of the Hassidic movement.

54

He was hounded by the Mitnagdim, as the opponents of Hassidism were called. Forced by them to leave several rabbinical positions, he wandered from place to place until he finally settled in Berditchev. Still, he refused to lessen his love for Israel, and his prayers for his people were so fervent that it was said that the soul of Rabbi Akiba of old had been reborn in him.

He directed his prayers to the Almighty, demanding that He stop the suffering of poor people at once and take better care of them. *"Derbarmdiger Gott!"* (Merciful God!) he would cry, and soon Levi Yitzhak was himself referred to as "The Merciful."

There was ample reason for this, judging by the beautiful stories that are told about Levi Yitzhak. He would hold up the services until the blacksmiths and tailors and shoemakers arrived at the synagogue. One Rosh Hashanah the rabbi raised the *shofar* to his lips, then hesitated, his eyes wandering to the rear of the synagogue.

The congregation became impatient but the rabbi kept looking at one of the congregants. At last he took a deep breath and blew the *shofar*.

Later, some of the people asked him why he had waited.

"It was for the poor tailor that I was waiting," said Rabbi Levi Yitzhak. "He cannot recite the prayers, for the only Hebrew he knows is the *Aleph Bet*. I saw his distress. The tailor was pleading with God, saying, 'O great God, I cannot recite the prayers because I am ignorant. But I know all the letters of the *Aleph Bet*. If I recite these letters over and over again, will You please take them and make up prayers as beautiful as those in the prayer book?'

"And that is why I waited," Rabbi Levi Yitzhak ended his explanation. "I wanted to give this man a chance to recite the Hebrew alphabet as many times as he wished."

In 1809 the gentle rabbi died. Over his grave his followers placed a simple marker. And until the Nazis destroyed the Jewish world of Eastern Europe, Hassidim would gather to pray at the grave of the rabbi who once prayed for his people.

THE RABBI AND THE BABY

HERSHEL OSTROPOLIER

HERSHEL of Ostropol was a jester whose pranks and quips brought grins and chuckles to the Jewish world of Eastern Europe. He was born in Russia to a very poor family. His father could give him no training and whatever Hershel tried went wrong. But his ability to laugh at himself as well as to cause laughter in others brought him fame.

For more than thirty years, from the 1770's to 1810, the leader of the Hassidim in the Ukraine was Rabbi Baruch of Tulchin. The son of Adele, the only daughter of Rabbi Israel Ba'al Shem Tov, who founded Hassidism, Baruch lived first in Tulchin, and later at Medziboz, the former seat of his grandfather.

He ruled with great power, traveling among his followers in luxurious carriages and collecting sums of money and presents from them. The rich looked to him for friendship; the masses sought his help.

His court in Medziboz, famous for its splendor, rivaled those of princes and Polish lords. His disciples dedicated themselves to his happiness. When the rabbi was sad and depressed, they thought it would help if he were to have a "court jester" such as Polish noblemen had. Hershel Ostropolier was chosen, and he performed his duties so well that he stayed with his master until Rabbi Baruch's death.

Hershel did not praise or flatter the rabbi. In fact he often irritated him by poking fun at his human weaknesses. Since the insults came from the lips of a clown, the rabbi laughed, and the Hassidim laughed, and all was well.

Hershel's bag of tricks included whopping lies, jokes, tricks, and witty sayings. For him, there was only one sin: to be dull. Because he dared to tweak the noses of the mighty, he became the hero of the lowly.

When a poor man dreamed of a get-rich-quick scheme, he usually had a rude awakening. But when Hershel's bubbles burst, the "pop" turned into a laugh.

He is the one who tried to sell a "rare" painting—a piece of blank paper in a cheap frame. "This shows the Children of Israel crossing the Red Sea," he told a rich purchaser. Where were the Israelites? "They have just crossed," said Hershel. The Egyptians? "They haven't arrived yet." But the sea! Where was the sea? "It was divided," replied Hershel. "Part of it went one way, part of it the other. The artist couldn't paint what wasn't there!"

Hershel and his audience are part of a world that has disappeared, but we have a record of his jesting and buffoonery, and when we laugh at his earthy wisdom, we are saying thanks to Hershel Ostropolier.

56

THE JESTER

AKIBA EGER

HE was a scholar descended from a long line of scholars, and by the age of 12 he had thoroughly mastered several volumes of the Talmud.

Born in Eisenstadt, Hungary, in 1761, Akiba studied at the yeshiva of his uncle, Rabbi Benjamin Wolf Eger, in Breslau. At the age of 18 he married and went to live at the home of his father-in-law, who gave him a fine library where he spent his days in study.

When a terrible fire in 1791 destroyed hundreds of homes in his city, Rabbi Akiba Eger accepted a post as a rabbi in the town of Markish-Friedland in West Prussia. In 1816 he became the rabbi of Posen and remained there for the last twenty-one years of his life.

In Posen his reputation flourished. When the government forbade the study of the Talmud, Rabbi Akiba Eger showed how highly the contributions of the Talmud to civilization had been praised by a number of Christian scholars. Impressed, the government abolished the order.

One winter he traveled all night to perform a good deed. On the way it began to rain heavily, and the carriage skidded into a ditch. The driver jumped down and pulled the wheels out of the mud. When he returned to his seat, Rabbi Akiba Eger offered him a pair of dry socks. The driver was puzzled, for the rabbi's baggage was locked in back of the carriage.

In the morning the driver saw that the rabbi's shoes covered his bare feet. The rabbi smiled and said, "How could I permit you to drive in wet socks while *my* feet were dry?"

Rabbi Akiba Eger visited the sick, always bringing little gifts. To the poor he gave of his own small income. When an epidemic of childbirth fever took the lives of many mothers, he appealed to more fortunate mothers to take the orphans into their homes. Once a week he visited each home to see that the children were well treated.

He became expert in the care of the sick. In the cholera epidemic of 1831 he gave advice on diet and sanitation, and was cited for loyalty and service by the Emperor himself.

His combination of great learning and deep modesty fascinated everyone. A dear friend, Rabbi Jacob of Lissa, once remarked: "How can he be so modest, when I know that he knows that I know that he knows?"

Before he died in 1837, he asked that his tombstone bear only these words: "Here lies Rabbi Akiba Eger, servant of God's servants."

But the people of Posen made one addition. They wrote: "Here lies *our rabbi*, Rabbi Akiba Eger, servant of God's servants."

58

'SERVANT OF GOD'S SERVANTS'

IN 1761, IN THE CITY OF EISENSTADT, HUNGARY...

RABBI MOSES, YOUR WIFE GITTEL HAS GIVEN BIRTH TO A SON!

MAY GOD GRANT THAT HE BE BLESSED WITH WISDOM AND UNDERSTANDING!

AS THE CHILD GREW...

I WAS THINKING OF SENDING YOU TO THE YESHIVA, AKIBA, BUT YOUR HEALTH...

FATHER, OUR FAMILY HAS ALWAYS HAD SCHOLARS. DO NOT LET ME SHAME THEM!

THE LAD STUDIED WELL. WHEN HE WAS 18...

REB ISAAC MARGOLIS, MAY I MARRY YOUR DAUGHTER?

YOU HAVE MY BLESSING, AKIBA EGER. BUT YOU MUST CONTINUE YOUR STUDIES.

AKIBA SPENT 10 HAPPY YEARS WITH HIS WIFE GLÜCKCHEN, STUDYING AND TEACHING. THEN IN 1790...

RUN FOR YOUR LIVES! FIRE!

THE CITY WAS DESTROYED.

WHAT WILL WE DO, AKIBA?

A CITY IN PRUSSIA IS SEEKING A RABBI. WE WILL GO TO PRUSSIA.

LATER RABBI AKIBA EGER BECAME CHIEF RABBI OF POSEN AND DEFENDED ITS JEWISH COMMUNITY...

THE GOVERNMENT HAS FORBIDDEN TALMUD STUDY IN JEWISH SCHOOLS, RABBI!

VENERABLE SIRS, I HAVE HERE THE FAVORABLE OPINIONS OF NON-JEWISH SCHOLARS ON OUR HOLY TALMUD!

HE WON IN COURT. THE ORDER WAS WITHDRAWN.

IN 1831, THE COMMUNITY WAS STRUCK BY THE PLAGUE.

YOU PHYSICIANS MUST VISIT THE SICK, RICH AND POOR! ALL FOOD MUST BE TESTED BEFORE DISTRIBUTION! WE WILL PUBLISH RULES FOR PROPER CLEANLINESS!

WHEN THE EPIDEMIC WAS OVER, HE WAS CALLED TO THE PRUSSIAN COURT.

I, EMPEROR FREDERICK WILLIAM III, THANK YOU FOR YOUR WISE LEADERSHIP. YOU HAVE SAVED YOUR COMMUNITY.

HE DIED IN 1837. HIS TOMBSTONE READ: "HERE LIES OUR RABBI, THE SERVANT OF GOD'S SERVANTS."

...THE NAZIS DESTROYED IT.

A MURAL IN THE CITY HALL OF EISENSTADT SHOWED HIM ON A MERCY MISSION IN POSEN...

...THE NAZIS DESTROYED IT.

BUT IN HIS WRITINGS AND HIS GOOD DEEDS, THE NAME OF RABBI AKIBA EGER...

...GREAT SAGE AND INSPIRED LEADER, WILL REMAIN ALIVE IN THE MEMORY OF OUR PEOPLE.

THE AMERICAN REVOLUTION

60

A STATUE on Wacker Drive in Chicago honors Haym Salomon, a Polish immigrant who is a symbol of American Jewish patriotism. The monument's central figure, however, standing tall and majestic, is General George Washington.

On the pedestal are inscribed words from a letter addressed to the Hebrew Congregation of Newport, R. I., a letter which says: ". . . The Government of the United States, which gives to bigotry no sanction, to persecution no assistance, requires only that they who live under its protection should conduct themselves as good citizens. . . . May the Children of Abraham who dwell in this land sit in safety, and there shall be none to make them afraid."

These words were written in 1790 by an outstanding champion of religious liberty and freedom, the first President of the United States.

Washington knew many Jews who joined the cause of the American Revolution. Though they made up only a small part of the thirteen colonies' total population of three million, they had rallied to his side far out of proportion to their number.

These early American Jews knew the meaning of suffering. Many had fled to the New World to escape the terror and oppression they endured as members of a persecuted minority. That is why they were among the firmest supporters of the rebellion against tyranny.

Some joined secret societies such as the "Sons of Liberty." Others helped with money, food, and military supplies. The financial sacrifices of a small number of wealthy Jews made the road to liberty an easier one to follow.

Jews did well in the fighting, too. They served in every colonial militia. One group, of Charleston, S. C., was even known as "The Jews' Company." There were many heroes, and the history of each is a story in itself.

On General Washington's personal staff as an aide-de-camp was Manuel Noah, father of Major Mordecai Noah. Others whom Washington knew well included David Salisbury Franks, entrusted by the General with important secret dispatches to envoys abroad in 1781; Colonel Isaacs Franks, confidential assistant to Washington; Major Benjamin Nones; and Moses Isaacks, at whose home Washington was entertained when he visited Newport.

When the Constitution was adopted and Washington was elected President, the six Jewish congregations in the country wanted to express their loyalty to him. They sent him letters of congratulation, one each from the congregations at Newport, Savannah, and Charleston, and a joint one from New York, Philadelphia, and Richmond.

To their good wishes, Washington replied with letters which have become a precious part of our country's heritage.

ROAD TO LIBERTY

SHORTLY BEFORE THE AMERICAN REVOLUTION, NEWPORT, R.I. NUMBERED AMONG ITS POPULATION OVER 1000 JEWS.

THEY HAD COME AS EARLY AS 1658, WHEN 15 JEWISH FAMILIES ARRIVED FROM BARBADOS.

THEY CAME BECAUSE NEWPORT, FOUNDED IN 1639, PROMISED, IN ITS CODE OF LAWS, THAT

All men may walk here as their consciences tell them Each in the name of his God.

EARLY SETTLERS FOUNDED CONG. JESHUATH ISRAEL (LATER THE TOURO SYNAGOGUE). THE SYNAGOGUE WAS DEDICATED IN 1763...

WHEN THE REVOLUTION BROKE OUT—

THE REDCOATS ARE COMING!

THE LEADERS OF THE JEWISH COMMUNITY MET.

WHAT SHALL WE DO, MOSES SEIXAS?

WE MUST JOIN THE PATRIOTIC CAUSE!

THEY FLED TO JOIN THE REVOLUTIONARY ARMY, AND THE BRITISH TOOK NEWPORT.

BY 1779 THE TIDE HAD TURNED, AND THE BRITISH HAD TO EVACUATE.

LET'S LEAVE 'EM A PRESENT!

SOMETHING TO REMEMBER US BY!

THEY DESTROYED THE DOCKS AND RAMPARTS OF NEWPORT. SOON THE EXILES RETURNED.

LET US GO TO THE SYNAGOGUE.

WITH YOUR PERMISSION WE'LL CONVENE THE GENERAL ASSEMBLY THERE, TOO.

IN AUGUST, 1790, THE SYNAGOGUE WAS HOST TO A GREAT VISITOR...

WE WELCOME YOU, PRESIDENT WASHINGTON!

I AM HONORED TO STAND BEFORE THE HOLY ARK.

WASHINGTON LATER WROTE A LETTER TO THE NEWPORT CONGREGATION, TODAY TREASURED AS THE MOST HISTORIC DOCUMENT IN AMERICAN JEWISH HISTORY.

To the Hebrew Congregation in Newport, R.I. The United States gives to persecution no assistance. May the children of Abraham sit in safety and there shall be none to make them afraid.

G. Washington

THOMAS KENNEDY

WE take for granted the idea of religious freedom in America. But matters were not always so, and the process by which American Jews achieved religious liberty was often a difficult one.

In Maryland, one of the original thirteen colonies, it was a Scotch Presbyterian who fought the battle for every man to worship God in his own way and still be a full citizen.

The Maryland constitution of 1776 required "a declaration of a belief in the Christian religion" for holding office in the state. In 1797 Solomon Etting, his father-in-law Bernard Gratz, and other prominent Jews of Baltimore petitioned the legislature to change this law.

Etting and Gratz spoke up stoutly, recalling the role Maryland's fifteen Jewish families had played in the American Revolution and pointing out, among other facts, that Jacob Hart, a Baltimore merchant, had raised $10,000 for Lafayette's soldiers. The bill was brought up in the legislature time and again but it failed to pass until Thomas Kennedy took up the fight.

Born in Scotland in 1776, Kennedy had come to Maryland in 1811. He did not live in Baltimore where about 150 Jews then resided, but in the western part of the state. His own feelings on the subject were very clearly stated:

"There are scarcely any Jews in the country from which I come and I have but the barest acquaintance with any Jew in the world. There are few Jews in the United States; in Maryland there are very few, but if there were only one, to that one we ought to do justice. A religious test can never be productive of any good effect. It may prevent the honest and conscientious from accepting an office, but the wicked and ambitious will not be stopped by so feeble a barrier."

The bill to make Jews full citizens was proposed as an amendment to the state constitution. An amendment had to pass two sessions of the legislature. It passed in 1822 for the first time. But in the next election, the fight was carried into Kennedy's home county. He was defeated for re-election and his "Jew bill," as it was called, failed with him.

In 1826 he campaigned for the "Jew bill" and was victorious. He thereupon introduced the bill into the legislature and proudly saw it carried for a second time. He had been bitterly opposed and he had fought only for the Jews; for all Christians, including Catholics and Quakers, were already full citizens in Maryland. In gratitude to Kennedy, the Jews of Maryland later erected a monument in his honor in Hagerstown, Md.

Thomas Kennedy of Maryland, sincere worker for the advancement of man, deserves to be remembered because of his dedicated service on behalf of religious liberty.

62

FIGHTER FOR HUMAN RIGHTS

IN 1797, IN MARYLAND, SOLOMON ETTING, BERNARD GRATZ, AND OTHER PROMINENT JEWS OF BALTIMORE CAME BEFORE THE LEGISLATURE...

OUR CONSTITUTION REQUIRES "BELIEF IN THE CHRISTIAN RELIGION" FOR HOLDING PUBLIC OFFICE!

MR. ETTING IS RIGHT! WE JEWS ARE THUS DEPRIVED OF CITIZENSHIP!

A VOTE WAS TAKEN TO CHANGE THE CONSTITUTION. AFTERWARD...

MR. GRATZ, THE BILL HAS FAILED TO PASS AGAIN.

ETTING, I SUGGEST WE GO SEE THOMAS KENNEDY.

THEY TRAVELED TO THE WESTERN PART OF THE STATE TO MEET A YOUNG STATE SENATOR.

WE HAVE HEARD OF YOUR LIBERAL VIEWS, MR. KENNEDY.

I WAS BORN IN SCOTLAND IN '76, THE YEAR OF FREEDOM!

I'M A PRESBYTERIAN AND I BELIEVE THAT EVERY CITIZEN MAY WORSHIP GOD IN HIS OWN WAY!

WILL YOU TAKE UP OUR CAUSE, MR. KENNEDY?

THERE ARE BUT A FEW JEWS IN MARYLAND. BUT IF THERE WERE ONLY *ONE*, WE WOULD OWE HIM JUSTICE! ...I'M WITH YOU, GENTLEMEN!

A LONG AND BITTER STRUGGLE BEGAN. IN 1822...

EXTRA! EXTRA! BILL TO MAKE JEWS FULL CITIZENS PASSES LEGISLATURE!

BUT AN AMENDMENT TO THE CONSTITUTION HAD TO PASS TWO TIMES! HIS ENEMIES WENT TO KENNEDY'S HOME COUNTY...

I SAY DEFEAT KENNEDY AND HIS "JEW BILL" TOO!

KENNEDY LOST. BUT HE MADE A COMEBACK IN 1826.

I THANK YOU FOR RE-ELECTING ME — AND THUS VOTING FOR THE PRINCIPLES FOR WHICH I STAND!

KENNEDY KEPT HIS WORD. ON FEB. 28, 1826...

MR. KENNEDY'S AMENDMENT HAS BEEN CARRIED!

PASSED FOR THE 2ND TIME, IT NOW BECAME A LAW!

AMERICANS OF THE JEWISH FAITH THANK YOU, MR. KENNEDY!

A RELIGIOUS TEST CAN NEVER PRODUCE HAPPY RESULTS. THAT IS WHY I FOUGHT!

THUS SPOKE A GREAT FIGHTER FOR HUMAN RIGHTS —

— THOMAS KENNEDY!

REBECCA GRATZ

64

A MEMBER of an American Jewish family famous during the 18th and 19th centuries as merchants and civic leaders, Rebecca Gratz was born in Philadelphia in 1781 and proudly continued the Gratz traditions.

She deserves to be remembered not only for who she was but for what she achieved in her own right. Gracious, wealthy and beautiful, she was also a woman of rare talents as an organizer and devoted worker for many charitable and religious causes.

She lived to the ripe age of 88 and by the time she died in Philadelphia in 1869, she was as well known for the legends that had grown up about her as for her worthy accomplishments.

People said that Miss Gratz had been in love with a Christian. She had refused to marry him, however, because of her faith, and she remained single all her life. Surely, considering her beauty, wealth, family background, and the fact that she was an observant Jewess, this might well have been the reason she did not wed.

The second legend is more firmly supported by fact. It is that Rebecca Gratz was the model for the character "Rebecca" in Sir Walter Scott's romantic novel about the Middle Ages, *Ivanhoe.*

Miss Gratz was a frequent visitor to Saratoga Springs, N. Y. While there, she met the American author, Washington Irving, who became engaged to Matilda Hoffman, a close friend of Rebecca's. Shortly before the marriage, Matilda fell ill with tuberculosis, and Rebecca nursed her during the last months of her life.

After Matilda's death, Irving made a trip to Europe to ease his sorrow. He visited Scott and spoke of Rebecca, of her devotion as a nurse, of her loyalty to her religion, and her refusal to marry a Christian. Scott was writing *Ivanhoe* at the time. It was published a few years later, and the heroine has many of the qualities of Rebecca Gratz which so impressed Washington Irving.

Miss Gratz threw herself heart and soul into social work. She brought up a family of orphans when their mother died. She organized the Female Hebrew Benevolent Society in 1819. She founded the Philadelphia Orphan Asylum and was its secretary for forty years.

Philadelphia was the home of the Protestant Sunday School movement. Miss Gratz, noting that many Jewish children were learning nothing about Judaism, established the first Hebrew Sunday School in America and was its president and superintendent for twenty-six years.

Rebecca Gratz helped the helpless and gave of herself for the good of others. Her letters and the record of her life show her wide interests and her allegiance to her people and to all humanity.

PHILADELPHIA LADY

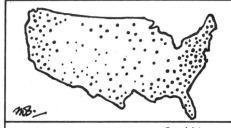

JUDAH TOURO

JUDAH TOURO was a living example of *tzedakah,* or "righteousness," in action. He distributed gifts in such number, and in so quiet a fashion, that many have still not come to light. But enough people were grateful in his own day for Touro to be provided with a tombstone which is a biography in brief. Here are the words, inscribed over his grave in the Newport, R. I., cemetery:

66

By righteousness and integrity he collected his wealth;
In charity and for salvation he dispensed it.
The last of his name, he inscribed it
in the book of philanthropy
To be remembered forever.

Judah Touro liked to boast that he was born in 1775, the year the American Revolution began. He lived to see his country grow bitterly divided on the question of slavery and he died in 1854 in his beloved Southern city, New Orleans.

His father, who had come from Jamaica to serve as the rabbi of the Newport congregation, conducted the first services in the beautiful synagogue which in 1947 was to be proclaimed by President Harry S. Truman a National Historic Shrine.

After an apprenticeship in his uncle's Boston counting house, Judah was ready for new adventures. In 1802, he went to New Orleans. The voyage from Boston took four months and was so wearying that Judah decided never to repeat the experience. He kept that promise.

He opened a store and traded in soap, candles and other New England imports. Keen in business, he invested his profits in real estate and ships, and grew very wealthy.

At the age of 40, Touro volunteered in the Battle of New Orleans against the British. Badly wounded, he was rescued by his very good friend, Rezin Shepherd, a non-Jew in whose home Judah lived for many years.

After a long recovery period, Touro turned to the main interest in his life— charitable deeds. He helped erect the Bunker Hill monument to Revolutionary War heroes. He founded the Jewish congregation in New Orleans. When dread yellow fever spread in New Orleans, he set up a hospital; it still exists and is known as the Touro Infirmary. He aided the Jews of China through the Hebrew Foreign Mission Society.

His interest in Palestine and in Hebrew was deep. He left a fund for a medal for excellence in Hebrew at Tulane University, and money to build the first Jewish houses in the new section of Jerusalem.

He never married and he had no heirs. But he made possible the establishment of asylums, orphanages, and libraries. Synagogues and streets are named for him in New Orleans and Newport.

He left a good name and a heritage of charity.

A HERITAGE OF CHARITY

MORDECAI NOAH

HE was a dreamer of dreams with an enormous appetite for action. Strange as that may sound, it nevertheless sums up the life and career of a fascinating figure in American Jewish history.

Ambitious and energetic, Mordecai Noah hoped to establish a refuge for the persecuted among his people. Of this hope nothing remains today but an inscribed stone in the Historical Museum of Buffalo, New York.

Born in Philadelphia in 1785, he was raised by his grandfather, who apprenticed him to a trade. But Mordecai had a nose for news, and he became a reporter at 15 and an editor at 25. He later led a many-sided life: he was editor of several New York newspapers, author of half a dozen successful plays, politician, and social leader. He was also a major in the New York State Militia, officer of a synagogue, president of Jewish charities, sheriff of New York County, judge of the New York Court of General Sessions, and surveyor of the Port of New York.

He was proudest of his appointment as United States consul to Tunis. His assignment was to ransom Americans taken prisoner by pirates and to work out treaties. When he was recalled, it was said that he had spent too much ransom money, but there were other rumors, ugly ones, with anti-Jewish overtones.

Noah never returned to government service. But he was not a man to sit still. On his travels he had seen oppressed Jews in Africa and Europe. In 1825 he had a vision of rescuing his people from world-wide oppression. Since Palestine was not available, he would build a city named Ararat on Grand Island, in the Niagara River opposite Buffalo.

He persuaded a Christian friend to buy the land and appointed himself the first Governor and Judge over Israel. On dedication day, clad in crimson, he led a long procession to the river's edge. But there were not enough boats to cross to the island. So the cornerstone was brought into a church and the ceremonies took place there.

Noah issued a proclamation inviting Jews from all the countries of the globe to settle in his new city. He also invited the American Indians, whom he believed to be the Ten Lost Tribes of Israel.

But no one paid attention to his proclamation. The refuge of his dreams remained a wilderness and the cornerstone was later given to the Buffalo Historical Society.

Noah died in New York in 1851. His dream was not fulfilled, but it bore the seeds of the Zionist movement, which was to blossom fifty years later and then flower into the reborn State of Israel.

MR. NOAH AND MT. ARARAT

IN 1813, AMERICAN SEAMAN WERE IMPRISONED IN ALGERIA. MEANWHILE, IN THE U.S....

YOU SENT FOR ME, PRESIDENT MADISON?

MR. NOAH, AS CONSUL TO TUNIS, YOU MUST FREE OUR MEN AND WIN RESPECT FOR THE UNITED STATES!

MORDECAI NOAH THUS EMBARKED ON AN AMAZING CAREER. EARLIER, AS A YOUNG BOY...

YOUR GREAT-GRANDFATHER CAME HERE IN 1733, AND I FOUGHT IN THE AMERICAN REVOLUTION. ALWAYS REMEMBER WHO YOU ARE, MORDECAI!

I WILL, GRANDFATHER!

IN 1812, NOAH MOVED TO CHARLESTON, SOUTH CAROLINA...

WE MUST RESIST BRITISH TYRANNY AS OUR FATHERS DID!

YES! HEAR! HEAR!

HIS BRILLIANT SPEECHES MADE HIM WELL KNOWN...

...AND CAUSED HIM TO BE SENT TO NORTH AFRICA BY PRESIDENT MADISON. ONE DAY, A U.S. WARSHIP ARRIVED...

WELCOME, COMMODORE DECATUR!

OUR NEW PRESIDENT, JAMES MONROE, WANTS YOU BACK IN THE U.S.!

YOU HAVE FREED OUR SAILORS...BUT ...THERE ARE OTHER REASONS.

IS IT BECAUSE OF... MY FAITH, COMMODORE?

SHOCKED, NOAH LEFT THE GOVERNMENT SERVICE.

HE BECAME SHERIFF OF N.Y., AND WROTE PLAYS AS WELL!

GREETINGS, MY FRIENDS!

MAJOR NOAH! PLAY WRIGHT! SHERIFF! JOURNALIST! WHAT ELSE WILL YOU DO, SIR?

NOAH SOON ANSWERED THAT QUESTION!

GENTLEMEN, I HAVE CHOSEN A HOMELAND FOR OUR OPPRESSED BRETHREN! GRAND ISLAND — NEAR BUFFALO, N.Y.!

WE WILL CALL IT MT. ARARAT! I MYSELF WILL BE GOVERNOR AND A "JUDGE IN ISRAEL!"

NOAH BELIEVED THE INDIANS CAME FROM THE TEN LOST TRIBES.

I INVITE YOU TO SETTLE WITH THE JEWS ON GRAND ISLAND!

ON THE DAY OF DEDICATION, SEPT. 15, 1825...

LET US NOW SAIL TO ARARAT!

UNFORTUNATELY NOAH HAD NOT PREPARED BOATS!

SO THEY DEDICATED THE CORNERSTONE WITH A 24-GUN SALUTE!

BOOM!

FIRE!

NO ONE EVER WENT TO "ARARAT." AMERICA ITSELF PROVED A LAND OF FREEDOM FOR ALL. BUT WE STILL REMEMBER...

...AN AMERICAN DREAMER AND PIONEER—MORDECAI MANUEL NOAH!

URIAH P. LEVY

70

IT is hard to imagine how anyone could lead a more varied life than did Uriah Phillips Levy.

He was born in Philadelphia in 1792 and he died in New York in 1862. In the years between, he was a sailor before the mast and an officer on merchant vessels and in the U. S. Navy. He was court-martialled six times but always restored to rank, and he died a Commodore, then the highest rank in the Navy.

At the age of ten, young Uriah ran away to be a cabin boy. He was master of a sailing vessel before he was 20. A mutiny left him alone and penniless in a foreign land. Somehow he managed to return home, accuse the mutineers, and have them convicted of mutiny.

When the War of 1812 broke out, he was commissioned a sailing master in the U. S. Navy. He was finally captured by the English and was held, with his crew, a prisoner of war in England for sixteen months.

In 1816, he was made sailing master on the *Franklin 74*. His enemies accused him of failing in his duty. He was court-martialled and dropped from the lists as Captain. But Levy fought back, and so impressed a court of inquiry that he was restored to his rank.

In the Navy, Levy met with double prejudice, as a Jew and as a sailor pro-moted from the ranks. He said his troubles were due neither to his humble beginnings nor to his fiery temper, but to the fact that he had remained loyal to the faith of Israel.

He certainly had his share of unpleasant moments. He fought a duel and killed his opponent. In Paris he heard a French officer and a civilian hiss the name of President Andrew Jackson. He challenged them both and forced them to apologize. During one of the six times he was court-martialled he happened to be in Brazil. Offered a post in the Brazilian Navy, he refused, saying that the humblest position in his country's service was preferable to royal favors.

He died just after the outbreak of the Civil War. His will asked that his tombstone record that "he was the father of the law for the abolition of corporal punishment in the United States Navy."

A great admirer of Thomas Jefferson, he purchased Jefferson's home, Monticello, and gave it to the people of the United States. He also presented to the U. S. Government a statue of Jefferson, which today stands in the Capitol.

In 1960, at Norfolk, Va., the Navy dedicated its first permanent Jewish chapel. It is named the Commodore Levy Chapel.

THE COMMODORE

ADOLPH SUTRO

ADOLPH SUTRO was an American Jew who left his influence on the West early in the history of its growth. Born in Aix-la-Chapelle, Germany, in 1830, he was educated at several of the best technological schools in Germany. At an early age he was placed in charge of his father's large woolen mills, but the German Revolution of 1848 made his family poor and the Sutros emigrated to America, settling in Baltimore in 1850.

In the same year, the discovery of gold attracted Adolph Sutro to San Francisco, where for the next ten years he sold tobacco and cigarettes. A few years later he was lured across the Sierra Nevadas by the discovery of silver in the Comstock Lode in Mount Davidson.

Sutro had studied mining, but he had never faced anything like the problems of the Comstock Lode. Miners were dying from the intense heat, for the temperature of the mine often reached 110°. The poisonous gases and the waters which flooded the mine caused many disasters.

Sutro developed an ambitious plan for a ventilating and draining operation. In 1864 he obtained the right-of-way for a tunnel through Mount Davidson. For fourteen years he worked on his project. He appealed to Congress for funds and traveled to Europe to raise more money when the grant was exhausted.

While Sutro was consulting experts in Europe, powerful opposition to his plan arose. His credit was stopped and his tunnel was ridiculed in the press. Sutro went to the miners themselves. He called a meeting of miners in Virginia City and won their support. The tunnel was begun in 1869 and completed in 1879.

With the mine operating successfully, Sutro moved to San Francisco. He collected a library of about 200,000 volumes and 135 rare Hebrew manuscripts. He spent $1 million for public baths and parks and furnished a band to play for the people each Sunday. He also gave the city an aquarium, and several statues and fountains. One of the richest men on the Pacific coast, he owned about one-tenth of the area of San Francisco, including Sutro Heights, which became a city property after his death.

In 1894, he ran for the office of Mayor of San Francisco. He said: "If placed in the Mayor's chair, I shall bring about an honest administration and yet save enough for a fund to beautify our city." He was elected.

Adolph Sutro died in 1898. His contributions to the science of mining and to the welfare of the average citizen have earned him a place of honor among America's pioneers.

THE MAN WHO DARED

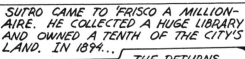

THE CIVIL WAR

THE Civil War has been called the Brothers' War. It was actually that in many cases, for Jews as well as non-Jews. Take the Jonas family, for example. Abraham Jonas, a friend of Abraham Lincoln's, had five sons. One was in the Union Army, but the other four fought for the Confederacy.

On the eve of the Civil War there were about 175,000 Jews in the United States. Many had made their way as peddlers, with packs on their backs, to all sections of the country. Jewish communities were fairly well organized, and the first representative American Jewish body, the Board of Delegates of American Israelites, had been formed.

In 1860, Lincoln was elected President and the slavery question boiled over. Southerners, who grew cotton, felt that slavery was necessary and proper. Since Northerners were not cotton growers, they could see slavery as the evil it was. Jews as a body took no action for or against slavery, although many prominent Jewish leaders stood in the front ranks of the anti-slavery movement.

On February 4, 1861, the South withdrew from the Union. The first shots were fired at Fort Sumter in South Carolina on April 12. The Civil War had begun.

North and South, Jews rushed to the colors, and many reached high positions. Judah Philip Benjamin, U.S. Senator from Louisiana, was appointed Secretary of State in the South and was called "the brains of the Confederacy." Senator David Yulee of Florida, who announced the secession of his state, had been the first Jew to serve in the United States Senate.

The first Surgeon General of the Confederacy was David de Leon, and the Quartermaster General was A. C. Meyers. Frederick Knefler attained the highest rank of any Jew in the Union forces. Volunteering as a private, he was repeatedly cited for bravery, and became a brigadier general, with temporary rank of brevet major general.

There were thousands of undecorated and forgotten heroes, and there were seven Congressional Medal of Honor recipients, whose recorded acts of bravery are a permanent part of American history.

The medalists were Leopold Karpeles; Benjamin B. Levy, for saving a vessel; Abraham Cohn, for rallying troops under fire; David Obranski, for gallantry at Shiloh and Vicksburg; Henry Heller, for bravery at Chancellorsville; Abraham Grunwalt, for valor in Tennessee; and Isaac Gans, for capturing an enemy flag.

In Washington today, souvenirs of Karpeles' life are displayed in the B'nai B'rith Exhibit Hall. In our capital, too, is the National Archives Building. On it is an inscription which links our lives to those who died so that our country might be whole again.

The inscription says: "What Is Past Is Prologue."

MEDAL OF HONOR

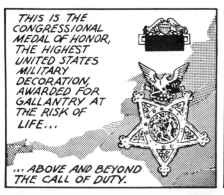

THIS IS THE CONGRESSIONAL MEDAL OF HONOR, THE HIGHEST UNITED STATES MILITARY DECORATION, AWARDED FOR GALLANTRY AT THE RISK OF LIFE...

...ABOVE AND BEYOND THE CALL OF DUTY.

AND THIS IS LEOPOLD KARPELES, FIRST AMERICAN JEW TO RECEIVE THIS GREAT HONOR.

BORN IN PRAGUE IN 1838, KARPELES CAME TO THE UNITED STATES IN 1850. TEN YEARS LATER...

DID YOU HEAR THE NEWS, LEOPOLD? THERE'S WAR BETWEEN THE STATES!

KARPELES LOST NO TIME...

I WANT TO VOLUNTEER, SIR!

FOR FOUR YEARS, KARPELES FOUGHT HIS COUNTRY'S BATTLE.

KARPELES, YOU'VE WON YOUR SERGEANT'S STRIPES TODAY!

THANK YOU, SIR. BUT... MOST OF ALL, I'D LIKE TO CARRY THE UNION FLAG!

FINE! WE'LL ADD ONE WORD— YOU ARE NOW COLOR SERGEANT KARPELES!

KARPELES THOUGHT HE'D REACHED THE TOP. THEN, ON MAY 6, 1864...

WE'RE LOST! LET'S GET OUT OF HERE!

LET'S SAVE OUR LIVES!

BUT SGT. KARPELES REFUSED TO LEAVE. MORE THAN THAT...

LET'S SAVE OUR COUNTRY FIRST! DON'T RETREAT! RALLY ROUND THE FLAG, MEN!

KARPELES BROUGHT NEW SPIRIT TO THE MEN.

—HE'S RIGHT!

—WE'LL FIGHT ON!

UNITED WE WIN!

—LOOK! THEY GOT KARPELES!

HE REFUSED TO YIELD THE FLAG...

DON'T...TAKE.. THE FLAG!

IT'S OVER, SERGEANT!

THE ENEMY HAS RETREATED!

LATER, SGT. KARPELES WAS CALLED TO WASHINGTON.

AT THE BATTLE OF THE WILDERNESS, HE RALLIED THE TROOPS AND CHECKED THE ADVANCING ENEMY. FOR THIS BRAVERY...

FOR THIS BRAVERY DID SGT. LEOPOLD KARPELES RECEIVE HIS COUNTRY'S HIGHEST AWARD, THE CONGRESSIONAL MEDAL OF HONOR.

DAVID EINHORN

76

THE slavery issue in the Civil War divided Jews as much as it did Christians in the United States. Those who dared speak out publicly against slavery were often very courageous. There was Rabbi Sabato Morais, spiritual leader of Congregation Mikveh Israel in Philadelphia. In spite of the pro-slavery feelings of some of his congregation and their attempts to prevent him from speaking, he uttered burning words of protest against slavery on behalf of Judaism.

He was one of a brave fraternity. The pioneer among Jewish pulpit leaders in this cause and the one who sacrificed the most was Rabbi David Einhorn.

A fighter since his student days in Germany, Rabbi Einhorn's anti-traditional religious views had brought him into conflict with Jewish leaders in his country and he was happy to accept an invitation to the pulpit of Har Sinai Congregation in Baltimore.

He preached eloquent sermons and edited *Sinai,* a magazine in German in which he wrote what he felt. His most important sermons and his views on the topics of the day, published in the columns of *Sinai,* spread his influence through the East.

When word of his sermons circulated through Baltimore, there were vicious mutterings against him. He had been proclaiming that slavery was contrary to the laws of God and the teachings of humanity. Most of the people in Baltimore were Southern in sympathy. He was told that there were plots against him. He went on preaching, writing, and taking sides against slavery.

The crisis came on the night of April 28, 1861. Soldiers, policemen, and friends warned Rabbi Einhorn that his name was on the list of those to be attacked. They begged him to display the Rebel flag from his housetop, but he refused. A volunteer guard of young men belonging to his congregation remained in his home, ready to shield him from assault.

At last he yielded to the pleadings of his friends to remove his family from the scene of danger. Silently, home and belongings were abandoned in a flight from the city, although Einhorn insisted on returning as soon as his family was safe. At last they reached Philadelphia, but return to Baltimore was prohibited under martial law and barred by his congregation, which demanded he change his views.

In Philadelphia he continued to be one of the warmest supporters of the Union. Rabbi Einhorn had not chosen an easy path. Once again the voice of an immigrant had spoken for the conscience of American Jewry.

THE RABBI WHO HATED SLAVERY

IN 1861, THE U.S. WAS SPLIT INTO TWO CAMPS...

CIVIL WAR BETWEEN THE STATES

IN BALTIMORE, RABBI DAVID EINHORN SAW ONLY ONE PATH TO TAKE...

AS JEWS WE MUST HATE SLAVERY!

AFTERWARDS...

MARYLAND'S A BORDER STATE, RABBI!

IT'S NOT SAFE TO PREACH AGAINST SLAVERY HERE!

GENTLEMEN, I WILL CONTINUE TO SPEAK THE TRUTH! SLAVERY IS INHUMAN!

BY MID-APRIL, THERE WAS RIOTING IN THE STREETS.

RABBI, I MUST SEE YOU. I FOUND A LIST...

WHAT KIND OF LIST?

HE LOOKED AT THE SHEET...

Abolitionists who must die:

Rabbi David Einhorn

I WILL NOT RUN AWAY!

WE'VE FORMED SOME YOUNG VOLUNTEERS. WE'LL GUARD YOUR HOUSE!

TIMES GREW WORSE.

WHAT IF THE MOB ATTACKED?

IF THEY STORM THE HOUSE... WHAT OF MY WIFE AND CHILDREN? A MAN MAY CHOOSE DEATH, BUT MAY HE SACRIFICE OTHERS?...

THERE WAS NO OTHER WAY...

EINHORN FLED TO PHILADELPHIA.

I WILL RETURN WHEN THE MADNESS IS OVER!

BUT A MESSAGE ARRIVED...

THE BOARD HAS DECIDED: YOU MAY NOT RETURN UNLESS YOU GIVE UP YOUR ANTI-SLAVERY IDEAS!

BALTIMORE WILL NEVER SEE ME AGAIN!

RABBI EINHORN KEPT HIS PROMISE. HIS VOICE RANG OUT FOR FREEDOM AND HIS WORDS LIVE IN THE PAGES OF AMERICAN HISTORY.

LINCOLN AND THE JEWS

FROM the time of his election until the unhappy hour of his death, Abraham Lincoln was a hero to many American Jews. He had overcome the handicaps of poverty and low social position. He had been a Moses to an enslaved people. He was the champion of the underdog.

When he began his journey from Springfield, Ill., to the nation's capital on February 11, 1861, he received a present from Abraham Kohn of Chicago. It was a flag of the United States. On it were painted the Hebrew words which encouraged Joshua in ancient times: "Be strong and of good courage . . . for the Lord thy God is with thee."

A close friend of Lincoln's was Abraham Jonas of Quincy, Ill. In 1864, one of Jonas' sons, who had fought for the Confederacy, was a Union prisoner of war. The father, dying at home, kept calling for his son, and the family turned to the President. The order went out at once: "Allow Charles H. Jonas a parole of three weeks to visit his dying father. June 2nd, 1864. A. Lincoln."

On another occasion, Lincoln stopped the execution of a Jewish soldier who had deserted to be at his mother's side during her last hours.

It was Lincoln who made it possible for the first Jewish chaplains to serve in the American armed forces by persuading Congress to change a law which required chaplains to be ministers of "some Christian denomination."

The most serious matter in which Lincoln helped American Jews was the one involving "Order No. 11." Issued by General U.S. Grant on December 17, 1862, it decreed that Jews were to be expelled from Tennessee, Kentucky, and Mississippi.

It was probably a move made under the pressure of traders who wanted to get rid of Jewish competitors. Grant later said that he had issued the order without thinking. But the damage was done. Jews as a class were branded undesirable citizens and traitors.

Three weeks later, Lincoln received Cesar Kaskel of Paducah, Ky., listened to the facts, and immediately had the order cancelled.

News of Lincoln's death on April 15, 1865, reached American Jews as they were conducting Passover services. The Festival of Freedom became a day of mourning. Altars were draped in black and Yom Kippur chants replaced happy holiday melodies.

Lincoln's body lay in state in Chicago's courthouse, under a canopy bearing David's lament on the death of King Saul: "The beauty of Israel is slain upon the high places."

In New York's Congregation Shearith Israel, on the Sabbath after Lincoln was killed, the prayer for the dead was recited for the first time for a non-Jew.

Lincoln had become an honorary member of the Jewish faith. It was the highest award American Jewry could bestow on its beloved leader.

78

'FATHER ABRAHAM'

ONE HUNDRED YEARS AGO, THE UNITED STATES WAS SPLIT IN TWO...

== THE CITY PRESS == 2¢

EXTRA! EXTRA! CIVIL WAR CONFEDERATE STATES BREAK AWAY FROM UNION

AS UNION FORCES MOVED INTO THE SOUTH, EVIL MEN STOPPED AT NOTHING TO MAKE A CROOKED DOLLAR...

"KING" COTTON CAN MAKE US ALL RICH, CAPTAIN!

WE KNOW WHERE WE CAN GET OUR HANDS ON IT!

BUT THIS TERRITORY IS CLOSED TO CIVILIANS!

WILL THIS HELP... UH... OPEN THE GATES? EH, CAPTAIN?

VICIOUS LIES REACHED THE EARS OF THE UNION COMMANDER...

GEN. GRANT, THIS CORRUPTION AND BRIBERY IS RUINING OUR MORALE!

AND THERE'S ONLY ONE GROUP RESPONSIBLE — THE JEWS!

THIS SHAMEFUL TALE WAS REPEATED AGAIN AND AGAIN...

...AT LAST, GEN. GRANT ISSUED A RULING KNOWN AS "ORDER NO. 11"

DEC. 17, 1862

All Jews are hereby expelled from this area within 24 hours. by order of Maj. Gen. U.S. Grant

PANIC STRUCK IN COUNTLESS COMMUNITIES!

CAN I SELL MY HORSE AND BUGGY?

NO SIR! THEY AREN'T YOURS ANY MORE. ALL JEWS GET ON THE NEXT TRAIN!

AT LAST AMERICAN JEWS RALLIED TO THEIR SELF-DEFENSE. IN PADUCAH, KY...

READ THE TELEGRAM YOU ARE SENDING TO PRESIDENT LINCOLN, CESAR KASKEL.

"MR. PRESIDENT, WE PROTEST THIS INHUMAN ORDER. IT WILL PLACE JEWS AS OUTLAWS BEFORE THE WORLD!"

KASKEL DID MORE; HE WENT TO WASHINGTON...

JEWS HELPED FOUND THIS COUNTRY, MR. PRESIDENT. WE HATE SLAVERY. DEMOCRACY IS IN OUR BIBLE!

THAT'S TRUE MR. KASKEL. NO ONE TOLD ME ABOUT ORDER #11.!

THE FOLLOWING LINES ARE RECORDED IN HISTORY...

AND SO THE CHILDREN OF ISRAEL WERE DRIVEN FROM THE HAPPY LAND OF CANAAN?

KASKEL ANSWERED IN THE SAME BIBLICAL MANNER.

YES, AND THAT IS WHY WE HAVE COME UNTO FATHER ABRAHAM'S BOSOM, ASKING PROTECTION!

AND THIS PROTECTION THEY SHALL HAVE! I WILL WITHDRAW THE ORDER AT ONCE.

THE ORDER WAS CANCELLED ON JAN. 7, 1863, MARKING A GIANT STEP FORWARD IN THE UNENDING AMERICAN BATTLE SEEKING LIBERTY AND EQUALITY FOR ALL!

MOSES MONTEFIORE

80

ON a fall day in 1883, a very old man sat hunched in a chair in a huge house in Ramsgate, England. A large velvet skullcap covered his head and he scarcely seemed to breathe.

A table held a stack of telegrams and letters. One of the telegrams had caused the old man to pause. It was from Her Majesty, Queen Victoria, and it read:

"To Sir Moses Montefiore: I congratulate you on entering into the 100th year of a useful and honorable life. Victoria Regina."

Sir Moses closed his eyes and thought back over the crowded span of ninety-nine years. It had been a full and happy life. . .

Born in Leghorn, Italy, in 1784, to a family that traced its origin to a small Italian town of the same name, Moses Montefiore was taken to England as an infant. His early manhood was spent in a business partnership with his brother Abraham. By 1821, he had amassed enough wealth to retire from the Stock Exchange.

He turned to developing new business enterprises and to helping people. He visited the Holy Land seven times, on each occasion founding hospitals and schools and aiding the poor. He bought land for agricultural enterprises and encouraged Jewish colonization. He established the first girls' school in Jerusalem.

He aided the Jews of Damascus when they were falsely accused of crimes, and visited the Sultan of Morocco to plead for better treatment of Moroccan Jews. Queen Victoria knighted him in 1837 and the same year he was elected Sheriff of London.

Audiences had been granted to him by the world's great—Queen Victoria, Queen Isabella of Spain, Napoleon III, the Shah of Persia, the Khedive of Egypt, and many others.

He had always remained a devout Jew. He attended the synagogue regularly. On his travels he had his own cook and special utensils.

A Torah Scroll traveled with him, and on the Sabbath he wore a ring engraved with the word "Jerusalem." A beloved figure, his picture hung in Jewish homes the world over.

On his birthdays, he would give to public institutions sums of money corresponding to his age, and on the Sabbath, when he handled no money, he would distribute meal-tickets to the needy.

The old man's eyes closed. Sir Moses fell asleep. . . .

Less than two years later, on July 25, 1885, Sir Moses Montefiore died. The Lord Mayor of London reported to his Council that "the most distinguished citizen of London" had passed away.

Sir Moses had no children, but the places and institutions that bear his name—Zikhron Moshe near Jerusalem, Sh'khunat Montefiore near Tel Aviv, Montefiore Hospital in New York, and others—are a memorial to his name and his noble deeds.

A MESSAGE FROM THE QUEEN

IN 1883, A VERY OLD MAN SAT OPENING BIRTHDAY TELEGRAMS.

AH! HERE IS ONE I DID NOT EXPECT!

HE HELD IT IN TREMBLING HANDS...

To Sir Moses Montefiore: Congratulations on entering the 100th year of an honorable life. Queen Victoria

HE REMEMBERED MANY THINGS... IN 1834, AT BROADSTAIRS, ENGLAND...

MOSES - HOW THE CROWDS MUST FRIGHTEN VICTORIA!

I'LL SEND HER THE KEY TO MY GARDEN, SO SHE CAN STROLL UNDISTURBED!

WHEN VICTORIA BECAME QUEEN IN 1837, SHE RETURNED THE KINDNESS.

I DUB YOU SIR MOSES!

BORN IN 1784, AS A YOUNG MAN HE ENTERED A LONDON COUNTING HOUSE.

HE BECAME ONE OF THE 12 JEWISH BROKERS LICENSED BY LONDON.

ABRAHAM, I HAVE SECURED THE ROTHSCHILD ACCOUNT!

WONDERFUL, MOSES, MY BROTHER!

IN 1821, MONTEFIORE RETIRED. HE VISITED PALESTINE 7 TIMES.

WHOM DID YOU HELP THIS TIME, MY DEAR?

HOSPITALS, POORHOUSES, TREE-PLANTING. IT IS OUR DUTY.

WHEN THE JEWS OF DAMASCUS WERE ACCUSED OF CRIMES, HE SAW THE SULTAN.

MY FRIENDS, I HAVE PROVEN THE CHARGES FALSE! YOU ARE FREE!

HOORAY, SIR MOSES!

HE SAW EVERYONE TO HELP OUR PEOPLE: ISABELLA OF SPAIN, NAPOLEON III, ALEXANDER II OF RUSSIA, THE SHAH OF PERSIA, THE KHEDIVE OF EGYPT...

HE LIVED THE LIFE OF A PIOUS JEW. ON THE SABBATH HE WORE A SPECIAL RING.

USALEM ירושלים

THESE THINGS HE REMEMBERED IN 1883...

HE DIED IN 1885 AT 101. THE NOBLE DEEDS OF THIS GREAT BRITISH JEW WILL ALWAYS KEEP HIS NAME ALIVE.

ISAAC ADOLPHE CREMIEUX

ONE of the most prominent Jews of the 19th century, Isaac Adolphe Crémieux was a French statesman, an outstanding lawyer, and a brilliant speaker.

He was born in Nimes, France, in 1796. His father was a merchant and a town official, and Adolphe was educated at the Lycée Impérial, where he and a cousin were the only Jewish students.

In 1817 he became an attorney, and soon won a reputation for his knowledge of the law. He entered the field of politics, became a member of the Chamber of Deputies in 1842, and was appointed Minister of Justice in 1848.

As a political leader, he pioneered in the introduction of important advances, such as the end of slavery in the French colonies, the abolition of death sentences for political crimes, and the establishment of trial by jury.

The services of Crémieux to the Jewish community began in 1827 when he started the fight that led to full citizenship for French Jews. Shortly afterward, he gained international recognition during the Damascus blood accusation trial.

In 1840, the Jewish community of Damascus, Syria, had been accused of killing a Franciscan friar in order to use his blood for religious ritual purposes. Jewish leaders were arrested and tortured. Crémieux of France and Sir Moses Montefiore of England came to Alexandria, Egypt, to plead with the government, for Syria at that time was under Egyptian rule. They succeeded in obtaining the release of the prisoners.

Meanwhile, Turkey had recovered control of Syria. Crémieux and Montefiore proceeded to Constantinople. The sultan was so convinced by their arguments that he branded the blood accusation an evil lie.

In his travels Crémieux saw at firsthand the poverty and misery of Oriental Jews. On his return to France, he formed the Alliance Israélite Universelle, a world-wide welfare organization which established a network of schools in the Middle East and North Africa. Crémieux became president of the Alliance and kept this post for life.

His attention had long been drawn to Algeria, which had been conquered by France in 1830. This event had brought 40,000 additional Jews under French rule. Jews had contributed to all the professions in French life. They had fought with all Frenchmen, cried Crémieux, for "liberty, equality, and fraternity."

On October 24, 1870, Crémieux's efforts bore fruit. The Jews of Algeria became full-fledged French citizens. It was a right that remained theirs even as they left in a tragic exodus when Algeria won independence from France in 1962.

On January 30, 1880, Crémieux lost his wife. She had been his beloved companion for sixty years. Both had often said that neither could live without the other. Within ten days Adolphe Crémieux was dead.

82

MINISTER OF JUSTICE

IN 1962, ALGERIA WON INDEPENDENCE FROM FRANCE... AS FOR ALGERIA'S OVER 100,000 JEWS...

THEY WILL BE RECOGNIZED AS FRENCH CITIZENS!

UNLESS, OF COURSE, THE WISH TO BE ALGERIAN NATIONALISTS!

IT LOOKED GOOD — ON PAPER. BUT THEY WERE CAUGHT IN TERRORIST CROSSFIRE...

... AND THOUSANDS LEFT THEIR NATIVE COUNTRY AS PITIFUL REFUGEES.

THEIR CENTURY-OLD CITIZENSHIP HAD BEEN DEARLY EARNED. IT ALL BEGAN IN 1840 IN PARIS...

ADOLPHE CRÉMIEUX, WE HAVE COME TO YOU BECAUSE YOU ARE A BRILLIANT LAWYER... AND A JEW!

IN DAMASCUS, JEWS HAVE BEEN ACCUSED OF MURDERING A CHRISTIAN MONK!

ANTI-JEWISH FEELING IS SPREADING LIKE WILDFIRE. HELP US!

CRÉMIEUX WENT TO SYRIA'S SULTAN...

YOUR IMPERIAL HIGHNESS, THE BIBLE FORBIDS JEWS TO USE BLOOD. THE CHARGE IS A VICIOUS LIE!

MONSIEUR CRÉMIEUX, I AM CONVINCED. I ORDER THE VICTIMS SET FREE!

HE RETURNED HOME IN TRIUMPH...

—WELCOME, ADOLPHE CRÉMIEUX!

—YOU ARE OUR HERO!

—YOU SHOULD BE MINISTER OF JUSTICE!

HE **DID** BECOME JUSTICE MINISTER, AND TURNED HIS ATTENTION TO ALGERIA.

MEMBERS OF PARLIAMENT, WHEN FRANCE CONQUERED ALGERIA IN 1830, 40,000 FRENCH JEWS CAME UNDER FRENCH RULE!

THEY ARE NOT TREATED AS EQUALS. YET DID THEY NOT FIGHT AT OUR SIDE FOR "LIBERTY, EQUALITY, AND FRATERNITY?"

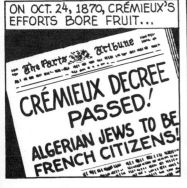

ON OCT. 24, 1870, CRÉMIEUX'S EFFORTS BORE FRUIT...

The Paris Tribune

CRÉMIEUX DECREE PASSED!
ALGERIAN JEWS TO BE FRENCH CITIZENS!

HE MADE MANY VISITS TO ALGERIA...

40,000 NEW FRENCH JEW! MORE THAN HALF THE NUMBER IN FRANCE ITSELF!

THIS WAS THE GLORY... A GIFT OF FREEDOM... FASHIONED WITH LOVE BY A GREAT ARCHITECT OF HUMANITY...

ADOLPHE CRÉMIEUX!

EMMA LAZARUS

MILLIONS of people have thrilled to the poem on the Statue of Liberty but how many know who wrote the verses or how they came to be placed on the statue?

The poet's name was Emma Lazarus. She was born in New York in 1849, a descendant of an early American Jewish family. Emma was given a good education and she began to write poetry while still young.

84

Her work attracted the attention of leading writers and poets, including Ralph Waldo Emerson, William Cullen Bryant, and Edmund C. Stedman. They told her she wrote well, but that she ought to show interest in her rich Jewish tradition.

It took a visit to Ward's Island in 1881 to stir Emma Lazarus to an awareness of Jewish life. There she saw victims of Russian persecution awaiting admission to the United States. She was so moved that she wrote an article for a magazine entitled "Russian Christianity versus Modern Judaism."

Meanwhile, the giant Statue of Liberty, a gift from the people of France, was nearing completion in Paris. A campaign in the United States to raise $300,000 for the pedestal for the statue was doing poorly.

Someone suggested an art exhibition and auction. Writers and artists were invited to contribute original works for the auction. Walt Whitman, Bret Harte, and Mark Twain were among those who sent original manuscripts. But only two authors produced something special for the occasion.

One was the 34-year-old poetess, Emma Lazarus. She refused at first, saying she could not write verses to order. But then she was reminded of the Russian refugees on Ward's Island.

Two days later, Emma Lazarus handed in "The New Colossus." It electrified the audience at the auction, and was sold for $1,500.

When the Statue was dedicated in 1886, Emma Lazarus was ill, and the poem seemed to have been forgotten. It was not until 1903, sixteen years after Emma's death, that the fourteen lines were inscribed on a bronze tablet and placed on the base of the statue.

Part of "The New Colossus" is also one of the first things a new arrival to the United States sees when he comes by air. Etched into a large marble block that faces the only exit air travelers can use after clearing customs at New York's International Airport are these lines by Emma Lazarus:

Give me your tired, your poor,
Your huddled masses yearning to
breathe free . . .
Send these, the homeless, tempest-tost
to me,
I lift my lamp beside the golden door!

'I LIFT MY LAMP...'

A SINGLE EVENT CAN CHANGE A PERSON'S LIFE. TAKE EMMA LAZARUS, BORN IN NEW YORK IN 1849...

EMMA, ARE YOU READY FOR YOUR LESSON?

YES, TEACHER!

SHE GREW UP SHELTERED FROM PAIN AND SUFFERING.

NOW, LET US READ "ROMEO AND JULIET." LISTEN CAREFULLY...

OH, I LOVE SHAKESPEARE'S VERSE, FATHER!

SHE HAD BEGUN TO WRITE POETRY HERSELF. WHEN SHE WAS 17...

A BIRTHDAY GIFT, EMMA! I HAVE HAD YOUR POEMS PRINTED!

HOW WONDERFUL!

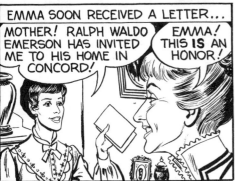

EMMA SOON RECEIVED A LETTER...

MOTHER! RALPH WALDO EMERSON HAS INVITED ME TO HIS HOME IN CONCORD!

EMMA! THIS IS AN HONOR!

THE FAMILY TRAVELED TO MASSACHUSETTS TO MEET AMERICA'S GREATEST WRITER...

SO YOU ARE MISS LAZARUS! YOU WRITE LOVELY VERSE, MY DEAR!

THANK YOU, SIR!

THEN, IN 1880, SHE CHANCED TO VISIT WARD'S ISLAND IN N.Y.

THESE FAMILIES HAVE ESCAPED FROM RUSSIAN PERSECUTION.

THEY ARE JEWS... MY OWN PEOPLE!

SHE BEGAN TO STUDY HEBREW AND TO EXPLORE JEWISH PROBLEMS. IN 1883, A VISITOR CAME.

I AM MRS. CONSTANCE HARRISON. AS YOU KNOW, FRANCE HAS GIVEN THE UNITED STATES A STATUE OF LIBERTY.

A GRACIOUS PRESENT!

BUT WE NEED FUNDS FOR A HUGE PEDESTAL. WE'VE INVITED WRITERS AND ARTISTS TO HELP. WILL YOU WRITE A POEM WHICH WE CAN SELL AT AUCTION?

I'M SORRY. I CANNOT WRITE ON ORDER!

THINK OF THE GODDESS OF LIBERTY HOLDING HER TORCH OUT TO COUNTLESS REFUGEES! PLEASE!

TWO DAYS LATER, EMMA WROTE A 14-LINE POEM. AT THE AUCTION...

"THE NEW COLOSSUS," BY EMMA LAZARUS... SOLD FOR $1500!

IN 1886, THE STATUE OF LIBERTY WAS DEDICATED...

...FROM OVER THE SEAS... BY SCULPTOR AUGUSTE BARTHOLDI...

...BUT EMMA'S POEM WAS NOT EVEN MENTIONED!

YEARS LATER, AFTER HER DEATH, THE BLAZING WORDS WERE INSCRIBED ON THE STATUE'S BASE. THEY HAVE INSPIRED MILLIONS:

GIVE ME YOUR TIRED, YOUR POOR.... I LIFT MY LAMP BESIDE THE GOLDEN DOOR!

EDMOND DE ROTHSCHILD

THE story of the fabulous House of Rothschild spans more than four centuries. The family took its name from a building at the sign of the "red shield" at Frankfurt-on-Main, Germany, where its fortunes were founded when Mayer Amschel Rothschild, starting as a trader in antique coins in the mid-18th century, became financial agent to a number of royal European families.

He left to his five sons a huge banking establishment and they soon fanned out to five European centers. By their influence and power, the Rothschilds were responsible for the industrial development of several countries.

Their achievements, sprinkled with "firsts," have filled volumes. Lionel financed Britain's purchase of the Suez Canal and in 1858 became the first Jewish member of Parliament. Nathaniel was the first Lord Rothschild and the first Jew to sit in the House of Lords. Ferdinand left a great art collection to the British Museum. Anthony was the first president of England's United Synagogue.

All the generations of Rothschilds have displayed remarkable family unity, and have been filled with a keen sense of responsibility to their fellow Jews.

It is said that during World War II Dr. Chaim Weizmann, meeting Lord Rothschild in a British air-raid shelter, asked him why his children were there instead of in the United States. Lord Rothschild replied, "Because of their last name. If I sent my three children over, the world would say that seven million Jews were cowards."

An outstanding Rothschild descendant was Mayer Amschel's grandson, a member of the French branch, Baron Edmond de Rothschild.

Edmond became one of the builders of modern Israel. In his lifetime, he donated 125,000 acres of land in Palestine, planted 50,000 trees, established health services, synagogues, and schools. He saved the first Zionist pioneers from financial collapse in the 1880's. He was known as the "Father of the *Yishuv* (Jewish Community)" and as the *Nadiv Ha-Yadua,* the "renowned philanthropist."

Edmond died in 1934, but his last wish was not fulfilled until the summer of 1954, when his remains and those of his wife, Baroness Adelaide, were laid to eternal rest in Israel.

When the coffins arrived from France at the Port of Haifa aboard the Israel frigate *Mivtah,* all ships in port flew their flags at half-mast, and a 19-gun salute was fired. The President of Israel and members of the Knesset were among the thousands who paid last respects to the Baron.

Thus Baron Edmond de Rothschild followed in the steps of the biblical Joseph, who made the Children of Israel swear that when they left for the Promised Land, they would take his remains with them.

86

THE BOUNTIFUL BARON

THIS COAT-OF-ARMS BELONGS TO ONE OF THE WORLD'S MOST FAMOUS FAMILIES—

— THE HOUSE OF ROTHSCHILD!

CONCORDIA INTEGRITAS INDUSTRIA

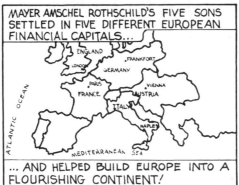

MAYER AMSCHEL ROTHSCHILD'S FIVE SONS SETTLED IN FIVE DIFFERENT EUROPEAN FINANCIAL CAPITALS...

ENGLAND LONDON FRANKFORT GERMANY PARIS VIENNA FRANCE AUSTRIA ITALY NAPLES ATLANTIC OCEAN MEDITERRANEAN SEA

... AND HELPED BUILD EUROPE INTO A FLOURISHING CONTINENT!

ONE DAY, IN THE 1880'S, IN PARIS...

WE HAVE AN APPOINTMENT WITH BARON EDMOND DE ROTHSCHILD.

YES, MONSIEURS. HE EXPECTS YOU.

ROTHSCHILD FRÈRES

YOU ARE NOTED FOR YOUR FINANCIAL GENIUS—AND YOUR GOOD DEEDS, BARON!

THE STRUGGLING COLONIES IN PALESTINE DESPERATELY NEED HELP!

BUT YOU KNOW, GENTLEMEN, THAT I AM **NOT** A ZIONIST!

ALL WE ASK IS THAT YOU COME AND SEE FOR YOURSELF, THEN—DECIDE!

ROTHSCHILD YIELDED. HE ARRIVED IN PALESTINE AND VISITED RISHON LE-ZION...

WHY DO YOU STAY ON THIS... DEAD SOIL?

BECAUSE IT IS OUR LAND — THE HOLY LAND! AND IT WOULD BLOOM... IF WE HAD A WELL!

THE BARON WAS INSPIRED BY THEIR ENTHUSIASM.

YOU **SHALL** HAVE A WELL. YOU HAVE MY WORD — **AND** MY CHECK!

IT **WAS** THE FIRST OF MANY GIFTS!

HE RETURNED A FEW YEARS LATER...

BARON DE ROTHSCHILD, THESE ARE YOUR GRAPES!

HAS HE SEEN THE WINE-CELLARS?

YOU ALONE HAVE DONE IT, BARON!

PLEASE STOP SHOUTING MY NAME!

THE GRAPES OF RISHON LE-ZION BECAME WORLD-RENOWNED!

EASY, THERE! THIS WINE HAS TO REACH THE U.S.!

PORT OF HAIFA

RISHON LE ZION

HE MADE THE LAST OF MANY TRIPS IN 1925...

AS I ONCE SAID GENTLEMEN, I AM... NO ZIONIST... BUT I HAVE SEEN WONDERS... WONDERS!

HIS GIFTS HAD ADDED UP TO OVER 70 MILLION GOLD FRANCS!

HE DIED IN 1934, A MAN WHO WAS "NO ZIONIST" BUT WHOM THE WORLD CALLED...

...THE "RENOWNED PHILANTHROPIST" (HA-NADIV HA-YADUA)— BARON EDMOND DE ROTHSCHILD!

ALFRED DREYFUS

ALFRED DREYFUS, a captain of artillery and the only Jew on the French General Staff, was accused in 1894 of selling military secrets to Germany. The plot against Captain Dreyfus was invented by a group of anti-Semites led by the real traitor, Major Ferdinand Esterhazy.

The German military high command, interested in stirring up hatred against the Jews, played its part. France was divided into two camps: the military, the Church, and the royalist party, versus the liberal republicans.

Tried by a military court, Dreyfus was found guilty and sentenced to life imprisonment on Devil's Island in French Guiana.

When Emile Zola, the famous French author, heard of the flimsy evidence against Dreyfus and of the shameful manner in which he had been stripped of his military decorations, he decided to investigate personally. On November 25, 1897, Zola began to publish a series of articles revealing the truth about the Dreyfus affair.

On January 11, 1898, the French courts cleared the name of Major Esterhazy. Enraged, Zola wrote "An Open Letter to the President of France," which has since become renowned in history under the title *"J'Accuse"* (I Accuse).

Zola's accusation against the French General Staff as partners in the crime against Dreyfus aroused a storm of charges and counter-charges. He was brought to trial for "insulting the French Army," and friends advised him to escape to London until France had grown calmer.

The miscarriage of justice was now being protested by others as well. Colonel Georges Picquart discovered the fact that the trial documents were forgeries. He demanded a review of the case by a non-military court. He was joined by the novelist Anatole France, the statesman Georges Clemenceau, and others.

The conscience of the French people was finally so stirred that Dreyfus was granted a new trial. By now everyone knew that he was innocent and it was expected that he would be freed. Nevertheless, he was found guilty again, though his sentence was reduced to ten years.

It was not until 1906 that Dreyfus was completely cleared and allowed to return to the army as a major. By then, Zola was dead, but he had seen the world recognize *"J'Accuse"* as a powerful instrument to help end anti-Semitism in official circles.

The Dreyfus case had a tremendous effect on many people. Among them was a young Jewish journalist named Theodor Herzl. Herzl had never before given much thought to Jewish problems, but now he had witnessed with his own eyes how evil a thing anti-Semitism was. So moved was he that he promised to dedicate his life to building a Jewish homeland in Palestine.

88

FOR TRUTH AND HONOR

THEODOR HERZL

90

THE dream of a Jewish State was born in the mind of a young lawyer, journalist, and playwright named Theodor Herzl. In his autobiography he tells us:

"I was born in Budapest in 1860. I remember my teacher saying that the word 'heathen' included idol-worshippers, Mohammedans, and Jews. . . We moved to Vienna in 1878, where I studied law and began legal practice in Salzburg. I would have remained there, but many doors were closed to Jews."

Herzl became a playwright and newspaperman. In 1891 he was sent to Paris by a Viennese newspaper. Shortly afterward, the Dreyfus case, involving a French Jewish military officer falsely accused of treason, was in the headlines.

Shaken and dismayed by such clear evidence of anti-Semitism, Herzl began to write his *Judenstaat* ("The Jewish State"). When he had completed the book, he showed it to a friend.

"He urged me to seek advice," Herzl later wrote. "He said everybody would think I had gone mad. I told him I would ask no one. I had to pass through a grave crisis. It was like dropping something red-hot into cold water. If that 'something' were iron, it would turn to steel. On that day my worries about the Jewish State began."

Herzl sought the help of Jewish leaders. He was turned down by some and not even answered by others. But the popular response to the publication of

The Jewish State kept growing, and Herzl assembled the first Zionist Congress, in Switzerland, on August 27, 1897. There Herzl said: "Maybe in five years, certainly in fifty, everyone will recognize the Jewish State."

For the next seven years, Herzl worked with feverish energy. He sought a "charter" for a Jewish State from Turkey, which ruled Palestine. He was received in audience by kings and ministers. His famous words, "If you will it, it is no legend," became the motto of Zionist hopes and activities for half a century.

In August, 1903, Herzl presided over a Zionist Congress for the last time. He was instructed to keep trying for a "charter," and to refuse the British offer of Uganda in East Africa as a home for oppressed Jews.

His labors had worn him out, and when he met with Zionist leaders in April, 1904, his face was pale and drawn. "One thing is certain," he said. "The movement will continue. I do not know when I shall die, but Zionism will never die. The Jewish State will come into being."

He passed away on July 3. On May 14, 1948, the prophetic statement he had made at the first Congress came true. One year later, on August 17, 1949, the remains of the founder of modern Zionism, flown from Vienna to Israel, were laid to rest on Mt. Herzl in Jerusalem.

FATHER OF THE JEWISH STATE

WHERE DOES THE STORY OF ZIONISM BEGIN? 2,000 YEARS AGO, WHEN THE 2nd TEMPLE WAS DESTROYED? PERHAPS. BUT CERTAINLY, THE DREAM TOOK ROOT WITH THE BIRTH ON MAY 2, 1860, OF THE FATHER OF THE JEWISH STATE-- THEODOR HERZL

THEODOR LEARNED OF ANTI-SEMITISM AS A SCHOOLBOY IN BUDAPEST.

WHO ARE HEATHENS? WHY, IDOL-WORSHIPPERS, MOHAMMEDANS, AND -- JEWS!

THE FAMILY MOVED TO VIENNA, WHERE HERZL STUDIED LAW. ONE DAY...

HERZL'S ALL RIGHT. BUT FROM NOW ON, THIS STUDENT CLUB WILL ACCEPT NO MORE JEWS!

HEAR, HEAR!

GOOD IDEA!

HE WAS GRADUATED AS A DOCTOR OF LAW IN 1884, AND MARRIED IN 1889...

WE'RE LEAVING THE LAW AND VIENNA, MY DEAR. A JEW CAN NEVER BECOME A JUDGE HERE!

HERZL BECAME A JOURNALIST IN PARIS. HE COVERED THE DREYFUS CASE.

DREYFUS IS GUILTY OF TREASON!

I AM AN INNOCENT MAN!

LATER... DEATH TO DREYFUS! DEATH TO THE JEWS!

THIS IS TERRIBLE! TERRIBLE!

TORTURED BY WHAT HE HAD WITNESSED, HERZL WROTE A BOOK...

I CALL MY BOOK "THE JEWISH STATE." HOW DO YOU LIKE IT?

DROP THE IDEA, THEODOR, IT WILL LEAD YOU TO THE MADHOUSE!

BUT HERZL PERSISTED. IN 1897, THE 1st ZIONIST CONGRESS WAS HELD IN SWITZERLAND.

IN 50 YEARS, EVERYONE WILL RECOGNIZE THE JEWISH STATE!

1st ZIONIST CONGR

HERZL PLEADED WITH RULERS OF MANY LANDS INCLUDING THE SULTAN OF TURKEY.

IF YOU GRANT US A CHARTER, YOUR HIGHNESS, WE CAN PURCHASE LAND IN PALESTINE!

EXHAUSTED BY HIS LABORS, IN 1904...

MY FRIENDS, IF YOU WILL IT, IT IS NO DREAM!

...HE DIED AT THE AGE OF 44.

HERZL'S LABORS BEGAN TO BEAR FRUIT...

HIS MAJESTY'S GOVERNMENT VIEW WITH FAVOR THE ESTABLISHMENT OF A NATIONAL JEWISH HOMELAND...

BRAVO, LORD BALFOUR!

...WHEN IN NOV. '17 ENGLAND ISSUED THE BALFOUR DECLARATION.

IN 1948, ISRAEL WAS BORN. HIS PROPHECY HAD COME TRUE. TODAY HERZL LIES ON A HILL IN JERUSALEM....

...BUT HIS MEMORY IS ENSHRINED IN THE HEARTS OF OUR PEOPLE THE WORLD OVER.

HERMANN SCHAPIRA

HERMANN SCHAPIRA had two great dreams. Both came true, but only after his death. One was the establishment of the Hebrew University, which came into being in 1925. The other was a plan to buy land in Israel which would belong to the entire Jewish people. The *Keren Kayemet Le-Yisrael* —the Jewish National Fund—was created in 1901, three years after Schapira had died.

Born in Lithuania in 1840, Schapira was ordained as a rabbi at the age of 24. Shortly afterward, a Hebrew book on mathematics which accidentally came into his possession sharpened his hunger for an education. He traveled to Odessa, to Berlin, and to Heidelberg to study. Despite great hardships—he worked in factories and slept on park benches—he won his doctorate at the age of 40.

He became an instructor and then an assistant professor of mathematics at Heidelberg University. At first he earned so little as a teacher that he had to repair clocks to support his family.

Deeply interested in Jewish affairs, Dr. Schapira became an active Zionist and a follower of Theodor Herzl. In Heidelberg, he founded "Zion," the first Jewish nationalist club in Germany. It was at the first Zionist Congress in Switzerland in 1897 that he laid the groundwork for the Jewish National Fund. He died a year later of pneumonia contracted on a Zionist lecture tour.

And what of the Jewish National Fund? It grew into a thriving, far-flung organization. It acquired land in Israel as the eternal possession of the Jewish people, it reclaimed and improved soil, and it prepared the country for new immigrants.

Through its land holdings and settlements, the JNF laid the foundations of the Jewish State, and its outposts were fortresses of Jewish military defense.

With the establishment of Israel, the JNF's work broadened. Of five million acres of land in Israel, only one and one-quarter million were being cultivated. The JNF turned the wilderness into good farming soil, provided land for new villages, gave newcomers employment in road-building and forest-planting, and taught settlers to grow more and better crops. The JNF also installed water supply systems and supplied plots for public buildings, schools, synagogues, and hospitals.

Through its little blue-white coin boxes, its Golden Book, the subscriptions and entries in the *Sefer Ha-Yeled* and *Sefer Bar Mitzvah,* the JNF has raised over $200 million, has bought almost a million acres of land, and has planted about 30 million trees.

If Professor Schapira could sit on the tree-shaded Tel Aviv street that is named for him and listen to these figures, how happy it would make his mathematician's heart!

92

THE PROFESSOR

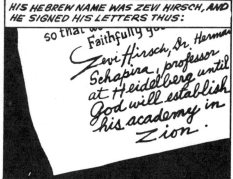

SOLOMON SCHECHTER

PICTURE a scholar in a smock, wearing a nose-and-mouth protector to keep out the dust of centuries, sorting thousands of fragments of precious paper. Around him are ranged rows of ordinary cardboard boxes labeled Bible, Talmud, History, Literature, Philosophy. He picks up a piece of yellowed paper or parchment, squints at it through a magnifying glass, and places it in the proper box.

The scholar is Solomon Schechter, bent over priceless Jewish manuscripts in the Cairo "Genizah." The Genizah is a loft in an old Egyptian synagogue in which holy books, too tattered to be used, were stored in olden times.

Schechter is busy with one of the most important discoveries in modern Jewish history. What road has led this man in the dust-coat to the capital of Egypt?

In the little village of Foscani, Rumania, where Schechter was born in 1850, he learned Hebrew at the age of 3, and studied the Bible and Talmud at 10. At the same time, the red-headed boy was full of mischief. He would never use a door when he could use a window, it was said of him.

After years of study in Vienna and Berlin he joined the faculty at Cambridge University. It was there that he identified a Hebrew fragment brought from Egypt as part of a long-lost Jewish work. Sensing that he was on the track of a big discovery, he packed and took a steamer to Egypt.

Among his finds in Cairo was more than half of the original text of *The Wisdom of Ben Sira,* an ancient book known to the world in a Greek translation. No one had ever before seen the original Hebrew!

His reputation grew and in 1902 he was invited to head the Jewish Theological Seminary of America. Dr. Schechter arrived to find a small training center for rabbis and teachers. Under his guidance, the Seminary became a leading institution of Jewish learning.

He stressed loyalty to Jewish tradition and introduced the riches of Hassidism to English-speaking Jews. He built up the Seminary library, which today has 200,000 Jewish books and 10,000 manuscripts.

At dusk on Friday, Dr. Schechter would welcome the Sabbath with boundless joy, for this was the day he loved most. Every Sabbath he stuffed his pockets with candies for his young friends in the Seminary synagogue. And on Sabbath afternoons, surrounded by children, he spun wonderful tales of Jewish life of long ago.

On Sabbath eve, November 19, 1915, Dr. Schechter died. Scholarly writer, brilliant lecturer, and strong personality, his influence was great on the development of Judaism in America.

94

TREASURE IN CAIRO

LOUIS MARSHALL

96

IN August, 1929, Jewish leaders gathered at Zurich, Switzerland, to draw up a constitution for the Jewish Agency, a body representing all Jewry in its struggle for a Jewish State.

At one of the conferences a short, stout, elderly man in a baggy suit came to the speakers' platform. The chairman, Dr. Chaim Weizmann, said only two words: "Louis Marshall!" The applause was thunderous.

Marshall told delegates he was not a Zionist. But now, he said, Jews of every opinion must forget their differences and stand united in support of Jewish rights in their ancient homeland of Zion.

The audience grew calm as he spoke, for Louis Marshall had a way with people. It had been that way for over half a century.

Born in Syracuse, New York, in 1856, Louis helped in his father's leather business by packing hides. In spare moments, he read the Bible and copied favorite verses on scraps of paper. His mother, a deeply religious woman, had inspired him with a lasting love for the Holy Scriptures. Later, when a friend praised him for an excellent speech, Marshall replied: "I said nothing; that was my mother speaking."

He was graduated from Columbia Law School and became an expert in constitutional law. He pleaded more cases before the Supreme Court than almost any other lawyer. But he never forgot his humble beginnings and his rich heritage. "Whatever concerns the Jewish people concerns me," he proclaimed.

He threw himself into pioneering movements with fiery zeal. He was a founder in 1906 of the American Jewish Committee; he spearheaded the work of the Joint Distribution Committee; he helped lay the groundwork for the Federation of Jewish Philanthropies of New York; he was active in the Bureau of Jewish Education of New York; he was chairman of the Jewish Theological Seminary of America and of Dropsie College.

Intolerance in any form was hateful to him. He fought for justice for Negroes, Japanese, and American Indians. He took no fee for such cases. As a delegate to the post-World War I peace conference in 1919, he saw to it that the rights of Jews and other minorities were written into the Versailles Treaty.

He refused to accept religious differences. A president of Temple Emanu-El in New York (Reform), he headed the trustees of the Jewish Theological Seminary (Conservative). In Paris, he prayed at an Orthodox synagogue.

The conferences in Zurich were a high point of his extremely active career. Shortly after his speech there, he died. Thousands came to pay silent tribute at his funeral. His good friend, Benjamin Cardozo, later to become a Supreme Court Justice, said, "How will we ever manage without him?"

The world knew what the question meant, for it recognized in this giant among men a spokesman for the human race.

SPOKESMAN FOR HUMANITY

IN THE 1860'S IN SYRACUSE, N.Y., A BOY HELPED HIS FATHER AFTER SCHOOL.

YOU'RE LEARNING HOW TO TAN HIDES WELL, LOUIS. WILL YOU BE MY PARTNER ONE DAY?

NO, DAD. I'M GOING TO COLUMBIA LAW COLLEGE AFTER HIGH SCHOOL.

SOON AFTERWARDS, LOUIS MARSHALL BECAME AN OFFICE BOY FOR NATHANIEL SMITH, A LAWYER.

WHEN YOU'RE NOT BUSY, YOU CAN READ IN HERE.

THANKS! I WANT TO KNOW ALL ABOUT OUR CONSTITUTION!

HIS READING CAME TO GOOD USE. ONCE, HIS EMPLOYER WAS IN COURT.

THIS CASE CANNOT GO ON TILL YOU PRODUCE THE SPECIAL REPORT ON THE ERIE CANAL.

BUT HOW SHALL WE FIND IT?

IT WILL TAKE DAYS TO LOCATE IT!

SUDDENLY, A YOUNG VOICE PIPED OUT:

I... CAN FIND THE REPORT. I READ IT JUST THE OTHER DAY!

WONDERFUL! WHO IS THAT LAD?

LOUIS MARSHALL BECAME A GREAT LAWYER, WITH MANY INTERESTS. BUT HIS CHIEF INTEREST...

I WANT TO HELP MY PEOPLE. THIS RUSSIAN BUSINESS IS BAD.!

MARSHALL WENT TO THE UNION OF AMERICAN HEBREW CONGREGATIONS AND TO THE AMERICAN JEWISH COMMITTEE.

THE U.S. HAS A TRADE TREATY WITH RUSSIA GOING BACK TO 1832.

WE KNOW. AND NOW RUSSIA DISCRIMINATES AGAINST AMERICAN JEWS.

THEY REFUSE PASSPORTS TO AMERICAN JEWS.

BUT WHAT CAN WE DO?

THE U.S. MUST BREAK THE TREATY!

MARSHALL CARRIED HIS FIGHT TO THE U.S. GOVERNMENT.

SENATE COMMITTEE ON FOREIGN AFFAIRS

NO. ALL AMERICANS MUST BE TREATED WITH EQUAL JUSTICE!

WON'T THIS LEAD TO WAR, MR. MARSHALL?

AT LAST, CONGRESS VOTED TO END THE TREATY. PRESIDENT TAFT SIGNED THE BILL.

IT IS MY PLEASANT TASK TO ANNOUNCE THAT THE 1832 TREATY IS DEAD!

MARSHALL CONTINUED TO WORK TIRELESSLY FOR JEWISH CAUSES, AND AFTER WORLD WAR I, AT THE PEACE CONFERENCE...

THIS PEACE CONFERENCE MUST WORK FOR THE RIGHTS OF ALL MINORITIES IN EUROPE!

JEWS AND NON-JEWS ALIKE WERE HELPED BY MARSHALL!

IN 1927, A COMMITTEE CAME.

A JEWISH AGENCY IS BEING FORMED, TO SPEAK FOR ALL JEWS. WILL YOU COME TO SWITZERLAND AS REPRESENTATIVE FOR THE NON-ZIONISTS?

THIS HAD BEEN HIS DREAM ALL ALONG. A GREAT JEWISH BODY!

HIS CROWNING MOMENT CAME WHEN DR. WEIZMANN INTRODUCED HIM.

I GIVE YOU-- LOUIS MARSHALL!

BUT DEATH OVERTOOK HIM BEFORE HE LEFT ZURICH. BRILLIANT LAWYER, LOUIS MARSHALL HAD BEEN A SPOKESMAN FOR THE HUMAN RACE!

ARTHUR JAMES BALFOUR

98

JOYOUSLY hailed by Jews the world over, the Balfour Declaration of 1917 came as the climax of twenty years of Zionist activity. The Declaration was the "charter" for which Theodor Herzl had worked so hard and so faithfully. It was an agreement with the nations of the world to permit Jews who needed a home to establish a homeland in Palestine.

Herzl had seen that without a charter large-scale settlement in Palestine was impossible. The country was under the rule of Turkey, and Herzl tried to obtain a charter from the Sultan. He was disappointed. He attempted to win the support of the German Kaiser and was turned away. The only country to show its friendship was England.

Herzl died before he could attain his goal. Years passed and World War I broke out. The Turks joined Germany, and the British determined to take Palestine from Turkey because it was important for the safety of the Suez Canal.

The war was going badly for Britain and it needed friends. Zionist leaders in England used whatever pressure they could. They also obtained the support of the United States, France, and Italy.

At last, on November 2, 1917, a letter was sent by Arthur James Balfour, British Foreign Secretary, to Lord (Walter) Rothschild of the Zionist Federation. It consisted of three sentences and said in part: "His Majesty's Government view with favor the establishment in Palestine of a national home for the Jewish people."

The man who signed this historic letter was a sincere friend of the Jewish people. His gentle spirit made him realize that the wrongs that had been done to Jews must somehow be righted. Even before the War he had been warm to Zionism. It was fitting that his name should be linked with the famous Declaration.

The Declaration won him tremendous affection. He was compared with Cyrus, who had granted the Jews the right to return to Palestine from the Babylonian Exile 2,500 years ago.

Balfour's services to the Jewish people continued even after the Balfour Declaration. In December, 1920, it was Balfour who, as a representative of Great Britain in the League of Nations, submitted the draft of the Palestine mandate. In 1922 he took part in the decisive meeting of the League in London, where the mandate was ratified.

In 1919, American settlers in Palestine established the colony of Balfouria. Six years later, Lord Balfour was invited to inaugurate the Hebrew University in Jerusalem.

Arthur James Balfour died in England in 1930. His name is remembered each year on November 2, a date that lives in Jewish history as Balfour Day.

THE DECLARATION

THEODOR HERZL, FATHER OF MODERN ZIONISM, DIED IN 1904. AT MANY MEETINGS...

WE MUST GET A CHARTER TO CREATE A JEWISH STATE IN PALESTINE!

BUT OTHERS BELIEVED DIFFERENTLY...

LET'S BE PRACTICAL! LET'S SEND MORE PIONEERS TO SETTLE IN THE HOLY LAND!

THUS WAS ZIONISM DIVIDED INTO TWO CAMPS!

A YOUNG LEADER SUGGESTED A COMPROMISE...

A COMBINATION OF BOTH APPROACHES WILL BENEFIT ZIONISM MOST!

YOU'RE RIGHT, CHAIM WEIZMANN!

THESE DEBATES WERE SUDDENLY STOPPED WHEN, ON JUNE 28, 1914...

EXTRA! EXTRA! ARCHDUKE FRANCIS FERDINAND ASSASSINATED!

... A HAIL OF BULLETS UNLEASHED THE FIRST WORLD WAR!

AT THIS CROSSROADS IN HISTORY, PALESTINE WAS UNDER TURKISH RULE. IN TURKEY'S CAPITAL...

GENTLEMEN OF THE PRESS! THE SULTAN ANNOUNCES THAT TURKEY HAS JOINED THE GERMAN SIDE!

PRESS ROOM

BACK AT THE BRITISH WAR OFFICE...

THE SAFETY OF THE SUEZ CANAL DEPENDS ON PALESTINE. WE NEED THE CANAL. WE MUST HAVE PALESTINE.

TURKEY

CYPRUS

RRANEAN SEA

CAIRO SUEZ PALESTINE

JEWS FLED FROM PALESTINE TO EGYPT. IN CAIRO...

MY NAME IS JABOTINSKY. LET MY PEOPLE FORM A JEWISH LEGION TO FIGHT WITH THE BRITISH!

PERMISSION WAS GRANTED!

IN THE U.S., SUPREME COURT JUSTICE BRANDEIS MET WITH PRESIDENT WILSON...

BRANDEIS, YOU'VE WON MY SUPPORT FOR A JEWISH HOMELAND!

YOU WILL NOT REGRET IT, MR. PRESIDENT!

AND IN LONDON, WEIZMANN CAME TO LORD BALFOUR...

DR. WEIZMANN, YOU'VE HELPED ENGLAND WITH YOUR CHEMICAL DISCOVERIES!

WILL ENGLAND HELP MY PEOPLE? FRANCE, ITALY, THE U.S.— THEY ALL APPROVE!

BRITISH FOREIGN SECRETARY

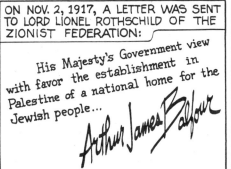

ON NOV. 2, 1917, A LETTER WAS SENT TO LORD LIONEL ROTHSCHILD OF THE ZIONIST FEDERATION:

His Majesty's Government view with favor the establishment in Palestine of a national home for the Jewish people...

Arthur James Balfour

THE NEWS WAS JOYFULLY RECEIVED. IN 1922, AT THE LEAGUE OF NATIONS...

BRITAIN WILL RECEIVE THE MANDATE FOR PALESTINE, TO CARRY OUT THE PROMISE SHE HAS MADE!

LEAGUE

AND NOV. 2 IS REMEMBERED FOR THE FAMOUS DECLARATION, IN A LETTER WRITTEN BY—

ARTHUR JAMES BALFOUR!

CHAIM WEIZMANN

100

THE Hebrew University in Jerusalem, the Technion in Haifa, and the Weizmann Institute in Rehovot—all these institutions of learning symbolize a fulfillment of the hope that one day the People of Israel and the Land of Israel would be united.

That was the dream of Dr. Chaim Weizmann. It kept up his courage on the long road from the little town near Pinsk, in Russia, where he was born in 1874, to Rehovot, Israel, where he was buried on November 11, 1952.

Chaim was the third of fifteen children. His father, a member of the *Hovevei Zion* ("Lovers of Zion"), a group that helped found modern Zionism, managed to give nine of the children a university education. Chaim's interest in science led him to the University of Freiburg, where he received his doctorate in science in 1900.

He soon was serving two masters—science and the cause of a Jewish homeland in Palestine. Then World War I broke out. His scientific discoveries made it possible for Britain to produce explosives at a time when they were desperately needed.

Dr. Weizmann refused a reward. "I want only a home for my people," he said. His efforts were crowned by England's Balfour Declaration, the first official recognition of the Jewish claim to Palestine.

It took twenty more years of hard work before he saw his greatest goal achieved. At the end of World War II, he appeared before the United Nations, pleading for the establishment of a Jewish State in part of Palestine to provide a home for the survivors of the destroyed Jewish communities in Europe. On May 14, 1948, the State of Israel came into being. Three days later, Dr. Weizmann was elected its first President.

The work had taken its toll, and his health was failing. On Sunday, November 9, 1952, with his dear wife Vera at his side, Dr. Weizmann died in Rehovot, just before his 88th birthday. Two days later, as sirens wailed in mourning throughout Israel, and across the globe in New York the UN General Assembly paused in respectful silence, Dr. Weizmann was buried in an olive grove that sloped eastward from his home toward the Judean hills and the city of Jerusalem.

Dr. Weizmann laid the cornerstone for both a university and a country. He built with the eye of a prophet and the hand of a master architect.

The hope he gave to the Jewish people—a hope translated into lives saved, universities founded, homes established, and a land reborn—will be an eternal monument to the name of Dr. Chaim Weizmann.

THE CORNERSTONE

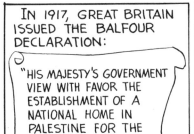

IN 1917, GREAT BRITAIN ISSUED THE BALFOUR DECLARATION:

"HIS MAJESTY'S GOVERNMENT VIEW WITH FAVOR THE ESTABLISHMENT OF A NATIONAL HOME IN PALESTINE FOR THE JEWISH PEOPLE."

WHEN CHAIM WEIZMANN HEARD THE NEWS...

WONDERFUL! I MUST RETURN TO PALESTINE AT ONCE!

WHEN DR. WEIZMANN ARRIVED IN JERUSALEM, GENERAL ALLENBY WAS STILL FIGHTING THE TURKS.

IS IT WISE TO COME HERE NOW? THOSE GUNS ARE DANGEROUS.

GUNS? I HEAR NO GUNS, GENERAL ALLENBY. BESIDES, I'VE AN IMPORTANT MISSION.

YES?

I WANT TO DO SOMETHING TO MARK MY VISIT, SOMETHING SYMBOLIC OF ZION.

GOOD! YOU CAN PRESENT A FLAG TO THE TROOPS.

NO, I WANT SOMETHING MORE. I WANT TO LAY THE CORNERSTONE OF THE HEBREW UNIVERSITY.

HEBREW UNIVERSITY. I SEE. WHERE?

ON MT. SCOPUS.

IMPOSSIBLE! IT'S UNDER FIRE. WHAT IF THE TURKS RETAKE IT?

LAYING THE FOUNDATION STONE WILL SHOW OUR FAITH IN YOUR VICTORY!

ALLENBY AGREED. ON JULY 24, 1918, AMID SHELLS AND BULLETS, BRITISH OFFICERS, ARABS, FRENCH AND ITALIAN OFFICIALS, RABBIS - AND CHAIM WEIZMANN GATHERED.

ON THIS DAY, 1800 YEARS AFTER THE DESTRUCTION OF THE SECOND TEMPLE...

...WE LAY DOWN THE FIRST STONE OF THE BUILDING WHICH SHALL BECOME THE HEBREW UNIVERSITY!

THUS DID DR. CHAIM WEIZMANN SYMBOLIZE THE RETURN OF THE JEWS TO PALESTINE, AND MARK THE FOUNDING OF HEBREW UNIVERSITY, WHOSE NEW CAMPUS NOW GRACES THE OUTSKIRTS OF JERUSALEM!

ELIEZER BEN YEHUDA

WHEN Eliezer Ben Yehuda began his work, Hebrew had not been used as a spoken tongue for nearly 2,000 years. By the time he died in 1922 at the age of 64, a new and youthful Hebrew was being spoken by a new and youthful country.

It would still take a quarter of a century for a Jewish flag to fly over Jerusalem, but he did live to see Hebrew being used in the schools, the courts, the theatre, business, and public affairs.

Ben Yehuda's dream had begun in Paris, to which he had come from Russia to study. It was there that he decided that his people needed a common language in order to regain Palestine. Hebrew was to be that language, but it had to be an up-to-date Hebrew.

In Paris, too, he discovered that he had tuberculosis. The doctors gave him a few months to live, and he slaved as if he had but a few hours. Ordered to seek a warmer climate, he went to Algiers, and then to Palestine.

In Jerusalem, Ben Yehuda published a magazine, *Ha-Tzvi* ("The Deer"), taught school, and began his great Hebrew dictionary. When he married, he made his wife promise to speak nothing but Hebrew to him or to any children they might have. When his son Itamar was old enough, they founded the first Palestinian daily newspaper, *Do-ar Ha-Yom.*

Ben Yehuda worked seventeen or eighteen hours a day. He wanted to keep Hebrew pure, to keep it from becoming a collection of foreign words written in Hebrew letters. Where then was he to get thousands of new words to suit modern life?

His method was to find a Hebrew word and build on it. For example, he created the word *meelon,* a dictionary, from *meelah,* meaning "a word." He manufactured *aveeron,* an airplane, from *aveer* meaning "air."

In 1909, he found a publisher for the first volume of his dictionary. It was unlike any that had ever been compiled. Each word was translated into French, German, and English. Origins, uses, synonyms, antonyms, shades of meaning were given. He listed 335 ways in which to use the word *lo,* meaning "no."

The labors were too much for one man. He died while explaining the word *nefesh,* which means "soul." Together with other experts, his second wife Hemda carried on the work, and the last volume of the *Complete Dictionary of Ancient and Modern Hebrew* was completed in 1958, a century after Ben Yehuda's birth.

A frail scholar, burning with an inner fire, had triumphed against overwhelming odds. Almost single-handed, Eliezer Ben Yehuda had created the language of modern Israel.

102

A LANGUAGE REBORN

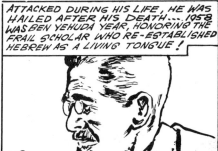

HENRIETTA SZOLD

BROUGHT up in a home which offered shelter and guidance to all who sought it, Henrietta Szold learned at an early age the meaning of humanitarian service.

Her father was a rabbi in Baltimore, where Henrietta was born in 1860. She saw her parents work for the freedom of the American Negro; she watched as Jewish immigrants from Eastern Europe were given a warm welcome in the Szold dwelling.

Miss Szold began her career as a teacher in a fashionable girls' school. In the evenings she conducted classes for immigrants. Her classes formed one of the first night schools for foreigners in the United States.

Half a century later, Mayor LaGuardia of New York bestowed upon her "the freedom of the city" in recognition of her Americanization work. Such labors as hers, he declared, had kept America from a new kind of slavery.

For many years she translated, edited, indexed, and proofread books for the Jewish Publication Society of America. One of her outstanding translations is that of Professor Louis Ginzberg's famous volumes, *Legends of the Jews.*

Her interest in Zionism grew naturally out of the idealism of her home. In 1893 she joined the Hevrat Zion, one of the earliest Zionist societies in the United States. She made her first trip to Palestine in 1909 and wrote home, "If not Zionism, then nothing."

In 1912, she changed the Hadassah Study Circle, to which she had belonged since 1907, to a national women's organization dedicated to improving health conditions in Palestine.

Hadassah brought doctors and nurses to what is now Israel; it started a nursing school, opened many clinics, and, with the Hebrew University, established the only medical school in Israel.

When the Nazis came to power in 1933, Henrietta Szold was determined to save Jewish children by bringing them to Palestine. She organized Youth Aliyah to rescue youngsters. Though Henrietta Szold never married, thousands of children, many of them scooped from under the noses of the Nazis, called her "Mother." Today Youth Aliyah cares for over 12,500 boys and girls in 250 special camps. They are children who have arrived in Israel without their parents or whose parents cannot keep them at home.

In 1935 a colony in Israel was named K'far Szold in her honor. In 1940, she was chosen by the Women's Centennial Congress as one of the world's hundred outstanding women of the past century.

She continued to be active into her 80's, and died in Jerusalem at the age of 84. The great organization she founded now has 318,000 members who carry on her pioneering work.

104

FOUNDER OF HADASSAH

ABOUT A CENTURY AGO, ON DEC. 21, 1860, AN AMAZING WOMAN WAS BORN-- HENRIETTA SZOLD.

WHEN SHE WAS EIGHT, THE FAMILY MOVED TO A NEW HOUSE IN BALTIMORE.

HENRIETTA, WHERE IS YOUR FATHER?

I'LL LOOK FOR HIM, MOTHER!

HENRIETTA FOUND RABBI SZOLD IN THE GARDEN.

SEE, HENRIETTA? THE BIBLE SAYS: "EVERY MAN SHALL DWELL UNDER A VINE AND FIG TREE." I'M PLANTING THEM NOW!

THUS SHE GREW UP WITH A DEEP LOVE FOR JEWISH TRADITION. IN 1881...

JEWISH REFUGEES FROM RUSSIA ARE ARRIVING BY THE BOATLOAD. THEY NEED EDUCATION.

WHY NOT OPEN A NIGHT SCHOOL FOR THEM, FATHER?

SHE BECAME PRINCIPAL. IN THE FIRST YEAR, 650 PUPILS ENROLLED.

WE WILL MAKE FINE AMERICAN CITIZENS OF YOU!

WHEN SHE WAS 23, SHE WAS CALLED TO PHILADELPHIA.

MISS SZOLD, WE'D LIKE YOU TO BECOME SECRETARY OF THE JEWISH PUBLICATION SOCIETY!

FOR 23 YEARS SHE EDITED, WROTE, HELPED THE J.P.S. PUBLISH ALMOST 100 VOLUMES!

THEN, IN 1909, SHE RETURNED FROM A VISIT TO PALESTINE.

MOST OF PALESTINE'S CHILDREN HAVE NEVER SEEN A DOCTOR! WHAT WILL WE DO ABOUT IT?

THE ANSWER WAS "HADASSAH," SO-CALLED BECAUSE IT WAS FORMED AT PURIM, AND HADASSAH WAS ANOTHER NAME OF ESTHER, WHO HELPED HER PEOPLE.

BY 1917, HADASSAH HAD 47 CHAPTERS AND 4,000 MEMBERS. IN 1920 MISS SZOLD WENT TO PALESTINE FOR 2 YEARS--

ONLY 3 DOCTORS FOR JERUSALEM'S 50,000 JEWS!

-- AND STAYED FOR 24 YEARS, TO THE VERY END OF HER DAYS!

IN 1933 BEGAN THE GREAT ADVENTURE OF HER LIFE!

WE'VE CONQUERED MALARIA AND TRACHOMA. PERHAPS I CAN GO HOME NOW.

THEN HITLER CAME. MISS SZOLD STAYED AND BEGAN A GIGANTIC PROGRAM--

WE MUST PERSUADE PARENTS IN EUROPE TO SEND THEIR CHILDREN TO US!

THE LIVES OF THOUSANDS OF BOYS AND GIRLS WERE SAVED THROUGH YOUTH ALIYAH!

HONORS POURED IN ON HER, BUT WHAT MOVED HER MOST WAS ONE VISIT...

EXCUSE US—WE HAVE COME TO SEE THE WAILING WALL—AND MISS SZOLD!

HADASSAH GREW TO 300,000 AND ITS HOSPITAL IN PALESTINE BECAME THE LARGEST IN THE MIDDLE EAST.

ON FEB. 13, 1945 SHE DIED—MOTHER OF HADASSAH WITH 318,000 MEMBERS IN 1,300 CHAPTERS, MOTHER OF 8,000 CHILDREN SNATCHED FROM HITLERISM, MOTHER OF A DREAM WHICH HELPED GIVE BIRTH TO ISRAEL!

RUFUS DANIEL ISAACS

106

FROM cabin boy to viceroy, from amateur boxer to England's leading judge: these were four of the rungs in the ladder climbed by Rufus Daniel Isaacs, one of the British Empire's outstanding Jews.

Rufus' studies consisted of a few years in a private Jewish school and less than a year at London's University College. The family fruit business seemed a boring prospect, so Rufus signed up as ship's boy on a vessel bound for India.

In 1884, at the age of 24, Rufus Daniel Isaacs had achieved success only as an amateur boxer, and he had paid for his lessons with a broken nose. As he was about to leave for a fresh start in Panama, his mother insisted that he study law. Older than most of his fellow-students and at a disadvantage because less than a handful of Jews had made a name in English law, Isaacs rose to the challenge.

Later, his son was to say of him, "He was at heart a man adventurous rather than ambitious, whose zest was for the battle itself rather than for the spoils of victory."

These qualities now began to reveal themselves. He soon became an outstanding lawyer, and at the age of 37, Queen's Counsel. Meanwhile, he entered politics, was elected to Parliament in 1904 and stayed in the House of Commons until he took his seat with the Lords.

In 1913, he was appointed Lord Chief Justice of England and created Baron Reading of Erleigh. With the outbreak of the First World War, Reading was a member of a commission that raised a loan of $500 million in the United States. He was created an earl in 1917 and returned to the United States as Ambassador Extraordinary.

Shortly after the war, Lord Reading was appointed Viceroy of India. The year was 1921. India was in a depression, Mahatma Gandhi was at the height of his influence, and England was an object of Indian hatred.

Lord Reading was warmly received, however. As a Jew, said the Indians, he would understand an Eastern people. He did succeed in introducing some advances in social welfare, and Lady Reading helped Indian women and children. Upon his return, Reading was made a marquess.

Proud of his Jewish ancestry, Reading became a leading Zionist and joined U.S. Supreme Court Justice Louis D. Brandeis in preparing an economic plan for Palestine. He also aided Jewish refugees from Germany after World War II.

When he died in 1935, the man upon whom so many honors had been conferred was buried, in accordance with his request, with a simple Jewish service.

'A MAN ADVENTUROUS'

RUFUS DANIEL ISAACS GREW UP WITH 8 BROTHERS AND SISTERS IN FINSBURY SQUARE, LONDON.

RUFUS IS TOO WILD, SARAH.

HE'S SO RESTLESS, JOSEPH.

IN SCHOOL AT BRUSSELS, IN LONDON, AT THE UNIVERSITY, IT WAS ALWAYS THE SAME...

DISMISSED AGAIN! NO SCHOOL WILL HAVE YOU, RUFUS!

RELUCTANTLY, THE FAMILY ALLOWED RUFUS TO LEAVE HOME...

ANCHORS AWEIGH!

...HE SIGNED UP ON THE INDIA-BOUND BLAIR-ATHOLE.

THUS, AS A LOWLY CABIN-BOY, RUFUS ISAACS FIRST SAW THE...

...INDIA WHICH HE WAS ONE DAY DESTINED TO RULE!

HE RETURNED TO LONDON AND OTHER ADVENTURES FOLLOWED— AS FRUIT MERCHANT, STOCK BROKER, AND EVEN AS BOXER!

C'MON ISAACS!

KNOCK'M DEAD!

AT LAST HIS MOTHER PUT HER FOOT DOWN.

YOU ARE DISGRACING YOUR NATION AND YOUR FAITH, RUFUS! SETTLE DOWN AND STUDY LAW!

RUFUS OBEYED. A REMARKABLE CHANGE TOOK PLACE.

THAT'S RUFUS ISAACS! FANTASTIC TALENT!

QUEEN'S COUNSEL AT 37!

IN 1913...

WE APPOINT YOU LORD CHIEF JUSTICE OF ENGLAND AND CREATE YOU LORD READING!

ON A VISIT TO THE U.S. IN 1918, HE WAS HAILED AS THE WORLD'S GREATEST JEW.

IN 1921 HE BECAME VICEROY OF INDIA.

LORD READING, WE MISTRUST THE BRITISH, BUT WELCOME YOU AS A JEW...

...FOR AS A JEW YOU WILL UNDERSTAND THE PROBLEMS OF AN OPPRESSED NATION.

THE INDIAN PEOPLE HAS ALL MY PERSONAL SYMPATHY!

HE RETURNED TO ENGLAND IN A BLAZE OF PERSONAL TRIUMPH.

EXTRA! LORD READING RECEIVES TITLE OF MARQUESS!

HE DIED IN LONDON IN 1935.

...THE FIRST JEW TO HAVE BEEN LORD CHIEF JUSTICE, AMBASSADOR, AND VICEROY— RUFUS DANIEL ISAACS, FIRST MARQUESS OF READING!

ORDE WINGATE

ORDE CHARLES WINGATE was a major-general in the British Army whose brilliant military leadership broke the grip of the Arab terror threatening Palestine in 1938.

A member of a Christian sect called the Plymouth Brethren, his religion taught him that the Messiah could not come until the Jews were restored to the Holy Land.

When he first arrived in Palestine in 1937 as a British intelligence officer, his lifelong study of the Bible made him feel as if he had come home. He visited all the Holy Places, learned Hebrew, and made friends with Jewish leaders in the cities and in the *kibbutzim.*

108

Wingate was there when Arab terrorists, helped by German and Italian spies, began their attacks on the Iraq-to-Haifa oil pipeline and on peaceful Jewish settlements. Despite the looting, the killing, and the sabotage, the British did nothing. In fact they arrested those caught defending Jewish settlements with arms.

With great difficulty, Wingate received permission from his superiors to restore order. Aided by the Haganah, the Jewish underground defense corps, he set up headquarters at Ein Harod, a *kibbutz* near Mt. Gilboa. There he trained his night patrols, numbering several hundred *kibbutz* veterans and hand-picked British soldiers.

Wingate taught them sniping, ambushing, and night attack. Within a year his crack commando force had smashed the Arab terror. Wingate said to his men: "You lack only weapons to be the most efficient and devoted soldiers in the world."

For his achievements, Wingate received the Distinguished Service Order. But he had irritated anti-Jewish British officials and he was recalled to England.

Wingate next fought in Ethiopia. He drove the Italians out and when Haile Selassie returned to claim his throne, he was met at the airport by General Wingate.

Then he was sent to Burma, where he was known as the Bible general. It is said that during one campaign he sent passages from the Bible as code messages to his men.

Using his original long-range penetration technique in Burma, he saved India from the Japanese in World War II.

He was inspecting the forward bases in the Burmese jungle when his plane crashed into a mountainside. Orde Wingate was dead at 41.

In Palestine, and later in Israel, Wingate continued to live as a legendary example of fearlessness and idealism. The mystics of the Mea Shearim section in Jerusalem believed that he was a forerunner of the Messiah. Near Haifa, on the slopes of Mt. Carmel, is the children's village of Yemin-Orde. Between Herzlia and Netanya is the Wingate Physical Training Institute. These are living memorials to a Christian who helped create the Jewish State.

THE COMMANDO

THE WARSAW GHETTO

110

A LONELY monument stands in Warsaw, Poland, marking the spot where the heroes of the Warsaw Ghetto fought and died.

This memorial in granite by sculptor Nathan Rappaport portrays a corner of a secret hideout where a group of Ghetto fighters fulfilled the vow of the underground movement in its last appeal to the outside world. "We may all perish, but we will not surrender. This is a fight for *your* dignity as well as ours. . . We will avenge ourselves for the crimes of Treblinka, Maidanek, and the other camps."

When the Nazis marched into Warsaw in October, 1939, they counted the population and found 360,000 Jews in the city. They then erected an eight-foot wall around the Jewish section and issued a series of decrees: "Jews coming into Warsaw must live within the walled area. . ." "All Jews of Warsaw must move into the Ghetto. . ." "All Jews in Warsaw are to be resettled in the East, beginning on July 22, 1942, 11 A.M."

Within two years all but 40,000 Jews had been swallowed by the death camps. The survivors formed the Jewish Fighters Organization, led by 23-year-old Mordecai Anilewitz. Arms were smuggled in and drills were held at night.

The first real test came on January 18, 1943. Nazi troops marched into the Ghetto to round up a batch of deportees. They were met by a hail of bullets and by bombs hurled by Jewish fighters disguised in German uniforms. The Nazis retreated in confusion.

On April 19, the final attack came. Nazi units marched in. The Ghetto was strangely silent. Suddenly a bomb fell on the leading tank. It had been thrown by a girl from a high balcony and it signalled the counterattack. Blue and white flags appeared on roofs. Posters on shattered walls declared: "We will fight to the last drop of blood!"

The Nazis returned in greater numbers. They threw fire-bombs, turning whole blocks into smoking ruins. They shut off the water supply. Observation planes directed the heavy artillery.

The Jews had only one possible remaining goal—to make the German victory as shameful as possible. The enemy was awaited in every doorway. Each defender took several Nazis with him when he died. On May 31, the Polish Underground Headquarters received a message from Warsaw. The Battle of the Warsaw Ghetto was over.

The night of April 19 had also marked the beginning of Passover. Thus the heroism of the Warsaw Ghetto has become forever bound with the historic meaning of the Festival of Freedom. If the world will only listen, the courage of the doomed fighters will serve as an eternal warning never to allow such a terrible tragedy to happen again.

WE REMEMBER OUR HEROES

HANNAH SENESH

IN the winter of 1945, an empty vessel was found drifting off the coast of Palestine. The passengers had vanished. "Illegal" immigrants, they had been smuggled under cover of night into the Holy Land. A few days later, a flag fluttered in the sand near the beached vessel. On the flag were these words: "The name of this ship is Hannah Senesh."

The name was fresh in the minds of all who had known her, for Hannah was gone but a short time.

She had been born on July 7, 1921, to a wealthy, cultured, and assimilated Jewish family in Hungary. At the age of 18 she came to Palestine to start life anew. In the agricultural school at Nahalal she trained herself for a life on the soil. But within her there burned an impatience, a sense of duty to do more important work.

She confided to her diary: "I feel that I have a mission. I don't know what my mission is, but I know that I have a responsibility to others."

Then Hannah heard that volunteers were being sought to parachute behind enemy lines in Europe. She knew at once that this was what she had been waiting for. On March 10, 1944, she left Palestine.

Parachuted into Yugoslavia, Hannah Senesh was assigned by the Underground to live with the guerrilla Partisans and to perform sabotage for the British as well as rescue work for the Jews.

Hannah did her job well, but she was anxious to cross into Hungary to rescue prisoners and to organize Jewish resistance. Besides, her mother still lived in the city of Budapest. On June 9, 1944, with the aid of Yugoslavian Partisans, she became the first to cross the border into Hungary.

There she fought with the Partisans until she was captured by the Nazis. She was thrown into prison, but her spirit remained unbroken. By bribing the guards, Hannah managed to carry on her rescue work even while behind bars. She made contact with friends on the outside and relayed information to fellow prisoners.

On July 11, 1944, Hannah was taken from her prison cell. No one was at her side to ease her pain. She refused to have her eyes bound, but stood straight and unmoving.

Several years before, Hannah Senesh had written a moving Hebrew poem:

> Blessed is the match that is consumed in kindling flame.
> Blessed is the heart with strength to stop its beating for honor's sake. . .

A pistol shot rang out. The young girl, who had left freedom to fight for it, was dead.

112

'BLESSED IS THE MATCH'

A STATE IS BORN

A TELESCOPED timetable of events forms a historic backdrop to the stirring drama enacted on May 14, 1948 (Iyar 5, 5708), when the State of Israel was born.

November 5, 1914: Turkey, of which Palestine is a part, becomes the ally of Germany in World War I. Palestine has a Jewish community of 80,000 souls. *November 2, 1917*: The Balfour Declaration is announced and later endorsed by the French and Italian Governments and by President Woodrow Wilson.

December 11, 1917: General Allenby enters Jerusalem at the head of the victorious Allied army and 400 years of Turkish rule come to an end. *July 24, 1922*: The Palestine Mandate, embodying the Balfour Declaration, is approved by the League of Nations. *May 17, 1939*: Following Arab riots, the British White Paper is issued, stating that the country is to become an Arab State within ten years, with a Jewish minority of 30 per cent of the population.

April 30, 1946: Britain rejects a report recommending admission of 100,000 Jews into Palestine. *April 2, 1947*: The Palestine problem is placed before the United Nations by Britain. *November 29, 1947*: The UN General Assembly votes, 33 to 13, for the partition of Palestine.

* * *

On the same day the Partition Resolution was approved in New York, the first Arab attack took place in Jerusalem. Britain had declared that the Mandate would end on May 15, 1948. Its civil and military administration began to leave the country without handing over the reins to anyone at all. The Arab population started to stream out of Jewish-controlled areas. The armies of the Arab States massed on the borders in order to move in as soon as the Mandate ended and "drive the Jews into the sea."

This was the setting against which Jewish leaders gathered on Friday, May 14, in the Municipal Art Museum of Tel Aviv. Distinguished visitors were in attendance and Haganah guards patrolled the area. At one minute after midnight, the Mandate would end. The Declaration of Statehood was to be made in the afternoon, in order not to violate the Sabbath.

As the clock struck four, David Ben-Gurion called the meeting to order. The assembly rose and sang *Hatikvah,* whose prophetic words were about to be fulfilled. Then Ben-Gurion began to read: "We, the members of the National Council, by virtue of the natural and historic right of the Jewish people and of the Resolution of the United Nations General Assembly, hereby proclaim the establishment of the Jewish State in *Eretz Yisrael,* to be called Israel."

Thus, 1878 years after the Roman legions had destroyed the Second Temple in Jerusalem, the Third Jewish Commonwealth was created.

114

MAY 14, 1948

MICKEY MARCUS

HIS real name was David, but in the tense days when he was on an undercover mission in Israel, his code name was "Mickey Stone," and Mickey it remained.

Mickey came to Israel in 1948 via Brooklyn, West Point, the Normandy airdrop and the Nuremberg courthouse. A scrawny kid out of Flatbush, he grew into a sturdy graduate of the United States Military Academy. He rose from government attorney to New York's gang-busting, prison-reforming Commissioner of Correction to commander of the Ranger school for Pacific jungle fighting.

In 1944 he slipped away from his U. S. Army desk in London to turn up as a volunteer paratrooper behind the Normandy beachheads. His last assignment before returning to civilian life was to gather hundreds of judges and lawyers for the Nuremberg trials of war criminals.

All this, it turned out, was in preparation for his meeting with destiny. When Israel was preparing for independence early in 1948 it issued a desperate call for Marcus. He believed in fighting for noble causes and he responded at once.

He flew over for six weeks and taught Israel's underground forces the techniques of West Point and instilled a respect for discipline into Israel's soldiers.

He returned home in time for Passover, but disturbing letters kept him from concentrating on his private affairs.

"I've got to go back," he told his wife. He promised to return by June.

He found Jerusalem cut off from the rest of Israel. There was hardly any food, or water, or electricity. Mickey Marcus helped the besieged city by building a secret road by-passing the Arab-fortified Latrun area on the Jerusalem-Tel Aviv highway.

On June 10, 1948, the road was ready. That night a truce was to take effect. Col. Marcus prepared to make a final tour of the battle lines. He had to be sure that the road to Jerusalem would be kept open.

He started to make his rounds. It was dark and it was quiet.

Suddenly, a shot broke the silence. A stray bullet fired by a nervous sentry struck and killed Micky Marcus.

The truce was declared on schedule. The Jewish sections of Jerusalem were in Jewish hands. The rest of Israel now had a breathing spell and a chance for victory.

The road he had built was named "Marcus Road." The hero, his action-rich life so tragically snuffed out at 46, was flown back to the United States.

Mickey Marcus was buried at West Point with military ceremonies, the only American who was killed fighting under a foreign flag to be so honored.

On his headstone is a brief but moving inscription: *Colonel David Marcus—A Soldier for All Humanity.*

116

THE WEST POINTER

DAVID MARCUS WAS BORN IN 1902 ON NEW YORK'S LOWER EAST SIDE AND RAISED IN BROOKLYN.

YOU WERE BORN ON FEB. 22, DAVID. PERHAPS ONE DAY YOU'LL BE AS GREAT AS GEORGE WASHINGTON.

I WANT TO BE A SOLDIER. I HOPE I'LL BE A BRAVE ONE!

THE AMBITION GREW WITH HIM.

IN 1924 HE WAS GRADUATED FROM WEST POINT.

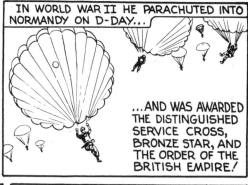

IN WORLD WAR II HE PARACHUTED INTO NORMANDY ON D-DAY...

...AND WAS AWARDED THE DISTINGUISHED SERVICE CROSS, BRONZE STAR, AND THE ORDER OF THE BRITISH EMPIRE!

HIS MOST TERRIBLE EXPERIENCE WAS VISITING THE NAZI CONCENTRATION CAMP AT DACHAU...

I WILL NEVER FORGET THIS!

HE RETURNED TO THE UNITED STATES. ONE DAY, IN JAN. 1948...

I'M FROM THE JEWISH AGENCY. ISRAEL WILL SOON BE FREE. WILL YOU HELP TRAIN OUR MEN, COL. MARCUS?

HE TURNED TO HIS WIFE...

I MUST GO, EMMA. I'LL RETURN...BY JUNE.

IT WAS A PROMISE HE WAS TO KEEP.

IN ISRAEL, MARCUS WAS WELCOMED BY YIGAEL YADIN, HEAD OF DEFENSE.

YOUR MISSION MUST BE A SECRET. YOU'LL BE KNOWN AS "MICKEY STONE."

FINE! WHEN DO WE START?

JERUSALEM WAS CUT OFF BY THE ARABS. A SECRET ROAD HAD TO BE BUILT.

WE'LL BE FINISHED TONIGHT, SIR. WATER, HELP AND FOOD WILL COME IN NOW!

GOOD! I'LL MAKE ONE LAST CHECK!

THE NIGHT WAS JUNE 10, 1948. A TRUCE WAS TO BEGIN NEXT MORNING. AS "MICKEY" MARCUS MADE HIS ROUNDS...

...A SENTRY'S STRAY BULLET FOUND ITS MARK!

ON JUNE 11, 1948, A TRUCE WAS DECLARED. ISRAEL PAID TRIBUTE TO A HERO.

WE NAME THIS JERUSALEM ROAD OF COURAGE "MARCUS ROAD!"

DAVID BEN-GURION CABLED EMMA MARCUS:

"HIS NAME WILL LIVE FOREVER IN JEWISH HISTORY!"

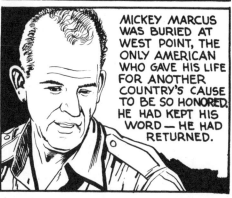

MICKEY MARCUS WAS BURIED AT WEST POINT, THE ONLY AMERICAN WHO GAVE HIS LIFE FOR ANOTHER COUNTRY'S CAUSE TO BE SO HONORED. HE HAD KEPT HIS WORD — HE HAD RETURNED.

STEPHEN S. WISE

LISTEN to words of guidance from a famous American rabbi: "I say this to all youth. . . . Let something so noble come into your life that it shall throw out everything low and mean. Work for the welfare of men and you shall have a richly satisfying adventure. *You are what your goal is.*"

These words were spoken by Rabbi Stephen S. Wise, who used his pulpit for more than fifty years to speak out against social evils and to appeal for clean, honest government.

All things Jewish were dear to his heart. He campaigned for a homeland in Palestine. He founded the Jewish Institute of Religion, which later merged with Hebrew Union College of Cincinnati. He helped set up the American Jewish Congress and the World Jewish Congress to study Jewish needs and rights in the U.S. and the world.

Stephen Samuel Wise was born in Budapest, Hungary, in 1874. His parents brought him to the United States when he was one year old. They prepared him from his earliest childhood for the rabbinate, and he became the seventh rabbi in direct succession in his family.

From the beginning he was an impressive spiritual leader. Tall and well built, with a high forehead, he had striking iron-gray hair and a rich baritone voice.

His first pulpits were in New York and in Portland, Oregon. Then, in 1905, came a turning point in his life. Temple Emanu-El in New York invited him to become its rabbi. Before accepting, however, Rabbi Wise wished to know if he would be allowed to say whatever he pleased in his sermons. When he was told that he would need the board of trustees' approval of the subjects on which he wished to speak, Rabbi Wise angrily turned down the offer.

So many friends supported his position that in 1907 he founded the Free Synagogue of New York which, because of his liberal views and orator's talent, became an important institution in American Jewish life.

Throughout his career he worked hard to create better understanding between Jew and Christian. "As a citizen," he once remarked, "I belong wholly to America. I give to it the utmost of my loyalty, the deepest of my love, the truest of my service. I thank God that my parents brought me to this country. I thank God that my children and my children's children have been born in America."

He died on April 19, 1949, at the age of 75, a happy man because he had lived to see one of his fondest dreams come true—the birth of Israel. Before he was buried, his children placed beneath his head a package of soil from Israel.

"You are what your goal is," he once had said. His goal was to be a rabbi who served mankind.

118

THE RABBI WHO SERVED MANKIND

STEPHEN S. WISE'S MIGHTY VOICE ECHOED AGAINST INJUSTICE ALL HIS LIFE. WHEN HE WAS A YOUNG MAN...

POLICE CLUBS MET MOTORMEN'S DEMANDS FOR HIGHER WAGES.

RABBI WISE DELIVERED A SERMON FAVORING THE STRIKERS. AFTERWARDS...

WE'RE SHAREHOLDERS IN THE COMPANY, RABBI.

YOU'RE MAKING ENEMIES!

I'LL ALWAYS SPEAK UP FOR THE WORKERS!

RABBI WISE HAD TO LEAVE HIS PULPIT. HE MOVED TO OREGON.

WE MUST CONDEMN CHILD LABOR AND OVERLONG WORKING HOURS!

OREGON BECAME THE FIRST STATE TO PASS CHILD LABOR LAWS. BUT...

WE LIKE YOU RABBI, BUT— WE CAN'T RENEW YOUR CONTRACT.

I'LL GO WHERE MY PRINCIPLES WILL BE RESPECTED!

BACK IN N.Y., HE FOUNDED A NEW CONGREGATION, THE FREE SYNAGOGUE. THEN, ONE DAY IN 1910 ...

IT'S THE TRIANGLE WAIST CO.!

THE WORKERS ARE TRAPPED INSIDE!

NEXT DAY...

EXTRA! 146 WOMEN BURNED TO DEATH!

LOCKED IN TO KEEP THE UNION ORGANIZERS AWAY! HORRIBLE!

FIRE 146 WOMEN WORKERS DIE EXTRA

ONCE AGAIN, RABBI WISE SPOKE UP.

PROPERTY IS GOOD, BUT LIFE IS BETTER!

AGAIN HE WAS CONDEMNED BY MANY.

HIS MOST DIFFICULT HOUR CAME IN 1919. MORE THAN 300,000 STEEL WORKERS WERE ON STRIKE. SAID THE U.S. STEEL CORPORATION...

...THIS STRIKE IS AN ATTEMPT BY COMMUNISTS TO CREATE REVOLUTION!

RABBI WISE STOOD UP FEARLESSLY...

I CHARGE U.S. STEEL WITH LYING AND VIOLENCE AND FORCE! AND NOW... I OFFER MY RESIGNATION!

THE CONGREGATION REFUSED! AND WISE'S NAME GREW EVEN GREATER.

FOUNDER OF A SEMINARY AND OF THE AMERICAN JEWISH CONGRESS, A ZIONIST AND FIGHTER FOR A JEWISH STATE, HIS FAME WAS INTERNATIONAL!

KONZENTRATIONSLAGER

IN NAZI CONCENTRATION CAMPS...

THE WORD "AMERICA" COULD MEAN DEATH. INSTEAD, INMATES USED A CODE WORD SYMBOLIZING FREEDOM:

STEPHENIA!

TO THE END, HE RAISED HIS VOICE FOR OUR PEOPLE...

PALESTINE MUST BE OPENED TO JEWISH REFUGEES!

HE DIED IN 1949, NOTED LEADER, GREAT HUMAN BEING—STEPHEN S. WISE!

SAFED

120

SAFED (pronounced *Sah*-fed; in Hebrew, *Tz-fat*) is the northernmost town in Israel. Its synagogues and holy places make it one of the most sacred communities in Israel's history.

It is also one of the most picturesque spots in the Jewish State. Its healthful climate and natural beauty have made Safed an attractive vacation resort. The main street, next to the stone bridge, leads down a lane to the artists' colony. Enter it and you are in a world of artists who have been drawn from many countries to the sun-drenched loveliness of Safed.

In the 16th century Safed was renowned as a great center of Jewish learning. It was here that Joseph Caro wrote the *Shulhan Arukh,* a detailed arrangement of religious laws. It was here that Rabbi Isaac Luria and his students pondered the mysteries of life hidden in the books of the Cabbala. Here, in 1580, the well-known Sabbath hymn, *Lekha Dodi,* was composed and sung. The first printing plant in Palestine and in all Asia was established in Safed, and through it the works which were created in Safed were spread all over the world.

Safed's cemetery, on the slope facing Meron in the distance, is the final resting place of many famous scholars. It is believed that under the steep hill lie Hannah and her seven sons, killed in Maccabean days because they refused to bow to the tyrant Antiochus.

Because Safed is the highest town in Israel, the top of its mountain was used in ancient times as one of the points for lighting a bonfire to announce the beginning of a new month and the arrival of the festivals. The first signal was given from one of the heights in Jerusalem, indicating that it was the time of the new moon. The message was passed from mountain-top to mountain-top. The Talmud tells us that a large, flaming torch made of wood and flax-fiber would be waved back and forth until an answering signal was received from the next summit.

It was in this sleepy town of synagogues and memories and scholars that a story of great heroism unfolded in our time.

At the outbreak of Israel's War of Independence the elderly people of Safed, left to the mercy of an overwhelming number of Arabs, were rescued by a handful of daring young Haganah soldiers who stormed the enemy positions and conquered the town in May, 1948.

Safed is built on the slopes of the mount called *Hametzudah,* the Citadel, after an ancient fortress that once stood there. Today the ruins of this stronghold are beautified with a park planted in memory of the young patriots who fell during the fight for freedom as they gave their lives to create the modern miracle of Safed.

A HANDFUL OF HEROES

THE SMALL TOWN OF SAFED, HIGH IN THE HILLS OF UPPER GALILEE, IS RICH IN JEWISH TRADITION.

ARTISTS, PAINTERS, AND SCULPTORS MINGLE WITH BEARDED HASSIDIM.

ITS SYNAGOGUES RECALL THE GLORY OF CENTURIES PAST, AND MANY RESIDENTS TELL OF WONDER-WORKING RABBIS OF OLDEN DAYS.

BUT IT IS THE "MIRACLE" OF 1948 WHICH FILLS ALL ISRAELIS WITH AWE.

OUR BRITISH TROOPS ARE UNDER ORDERS TO LEAVE THE AREA. FOR YOUR SAFETY, COME WITH US!

WE NUMBER 1,700. THERE ARE ONLY 12,000 ARABS HERE...HMN. WE SHALL STAY.

WELL, YOU CAN'T SAY I DIDN'T WARN YOU.

THE BRITISH GARRISON PULLED OUT ON APRIL 16, GIVING THE ARABS THE POLICE STATION AND A MOUNTAIN FORTRESS.

A SMALL GROUP OF HAGANAH MEN, LED BY YIGAL ALLON, CROSSED THE ARAB LINES DESPITE THE SNIPING AND GRENADE-THROWING.

SAFED CONTROLS THE ROADS TO EASTERN GALILEE. WE'VE GOT TO HOLD IT!

YOU'RE RIGHT, YIGAL!

AT NIGHT THEY REPAIRED ROADS AND BRIDGES.

FIX THIS BRIDGE WELL. TOMORROW NIGHT WE MOVE. HERE'S MY PLAN...

ON THE NIGHT OF MAY 10...

...PICKED MEN STORMED THE TWO ARAB STRONGHOLDS.

...AND FOUGHT IN THE STREETS...

THE ENEMY NUMBERS THOUSANDS! WE MUST ESCAPE!

AND THE ARABS FLED IN PANIC...

THEY'RE USING THE ONE ROUTE WE LEFT OPEN! OUR PLAN IS WORKING!

NEXT DAY, THERE WAS DANCING IN THE STREETS...

THE "MIRACLE OF SAFED" HAD BECOME PART OF ISRAEL'S HISTORY!

DEGANIA

ISRAEL'S chief *k'vutzot,* or communal settlements, are in Emek Jezreel and the Jordan Valley. They are situated on land bought by the Jewish National Fund, land that can never be sold by individuals, for it belongs to the Jewish people.

Degania, just south of the Sea of Galilee, is called the "mother of *k'vutzot*" because it was founded over fifty years ago. The area then was desolate and full of swamps. In a tropical climate, open to the attacks of looting Bedouins, and with no experience in agriculture, the hardy settlers needed luck and determination.

Slowly the farmers worked out the methods that best suited local conditions. Degania served as an example and training school for hundreds of young pioneers who came with the dream of making Palestine as fruitful as it had been in ancient times.

A man who blazed the trail at Degania was A. D. Gordon, who left a comfortable home in Russia at the age of 50 to pioneer in Palestine. He settled in Degania and inspired the *halutzim* with his philosophy. He believed that only through physical labor could Jews redeem the Holy Land. Degania honors his memory with a museum of natural science called Bet Gordon. Above the entrance to the auditorium next to the museum are Gordon's words: "And you shall learn from nature."

Newcomers work at Degania for about a year, after which the group decides on their fitness for membership. Sometimes, members leave to establish a new *k'vutzah.*

Degania grows vegetables, bananas, grapefruit, and grain. Its dairies and hen houses are models of cleanliness and modern equipment.

Near its long avenue lined with tall cypress trees is Degania's cemetery. There lie some of the first pioneers who sacrificed their lives in building the colony. But one can see recent graves, too. Buried in them are brave defenders who held back the Syrians from invading Israel in the War of Independence.

Degania was a frontier fortress then. When the Syrians approached, the settlers had only a few guns and some Molotov cocktails—bottles of kerosene lit by burning rags. Equipped with these scanty arms, the young fighters drove the heavily armored enemy back to their border.

The first enemy tank that was stopped is still astride the defensive ditch at the entrance to Degania. It is a symbol of heroic resistance. On Independence Day of 1952, a special stamp was issued by Israel to commemorate Degania's victory.

THE TANK WAS STOPPED

THE VISITOR TO DEGANIA, BEAUTIFUL SETTLEMENT IN THE JORDAN VALLEY, IS GIVEN A WARM WELCOME.

WON'T YOU BE OUR GUESTS FOR DINNER?

BUT ALWAYS, THERE IS A QUESTION ASKED FIRST.

WHY DO YOU KEEP THIS RUSTY TANK HERE?

AH, THAT TANK TELLS A STORY!

DEGANIA IS THE FIRST OF ISRAEL'S COLLECTIVE SETTLEMENTS. IT WAS FOUNDED OVER FIFTY YEARS AGO.

"ON MAY 15, 1948, ONE DAY AFTER ISRAEL WAS ESTABLISHED..."

WORD JUST CAME. THE SYRIANS ARE ATTACKING!

IF THEY TAKE DEGANIA, THEY'LL CONTROL THE SEA OF GALILEE AND THE JORDAN VALLEY!

A MESSENGER WAS SENT TO YIGAEL YADIN, CHIEF OF STAFF...

WE'VE GOT RIFLES, BUT THEY WON'T STOP A TANK!

WE CAN'T HELP YOU, UNFORTUNATELY. GO BACK. LET THE SYRIANS COME. YOU'LL DEFEAT THEM.

YADIN COUNTED ON TRADITIONAL DEGANIA COURAGE; BACK IN THE COLONY...

THE SYRIANS HAVE BROKEN THROUGH THE OUTER DEFENSES!

WE'VE GOT TO STOP THE TANKS!

BUT HOW?

WE'D LIKE TO VOLUNTEER FOR THE JOB!

YOU?! YOU'LL BE KILLED!

WE'LL TAKE OUR CHANCES. SEE WHAT WE'VE GOT!

MOLOTOV COCKTAILS-- HOME-MADE BOMBS!

THE MINUTES SPED BY...

LET THEM GET CLOSER. WE CAN'T AFFORD TO MISS!

NOW!

WE GOT THE FIRST TANK!

THE REST ARE RETREATING!

DEGANIA WAS SAVED. TODAY THE RUSTY TANK STANDS IN PEACEFUL DEGANIA...

...REMINDING ALL WHO SEE IT OF A MIRACLE OF MODERN TIMES.

ALBERT EINSTEIN

ALBERT EINSTEIN devoted as much time to helping his fellow man as to expanding the frontiers of knowledge.

No scientist received as many honors in his lifetime as did Einstein. But he had known pain and suffering too. As a lad of 6 he met anti-Semitism in the form of a bigoted and ignorant teacher in his German school. He never forgot this experience and, as he grew older, he stubbornly fought injustice.

Even as a boy he was always asking questions. When he was ten, Albert asked his uncle, "What is algebra?"

"Algebra," replied the uncle, "is a lazy kind of arithmetic. When you don't know something, you call it x and then look for it."

Einstein spent his life trying to solve the unknown. In the early 1900's, the world of science was aroused by the genius shown in his essays on relativity. He was invited to teach at several universities and won a Nobel Prize in 1921.

World War I had reminded Einstein that he was a Jew. After the war, students interrupted his lectures at the Prussian Academy with shouts of "Throw the Jew out!"

When the Nazis came to power, they looted his house and offered a reward for anyone who would "silence" him. Fortunately, he happened to be in Belgium, not in Germany. He was spirited to the United States by friends in October, 1933.

He had last been in America in December, 1930, when he had been given an overwhelming reception. He visited the Riverside Church in Manhattan where the figures of many personalities—philosophers, scientists, kings—had lately been carved in limestone. Einstein was the *only living man* represented in this gallery of greats.

On his way across the country, he stopped at the Grand Canyon. The Hopi Indians wanted to make him a chieftain, but they were puzzled about his profession.

"What's his business?" the Hopis asked.

"He invented the theory of relativity," they were told.

"Good," the Hopis replied. "We will call him 'Great Relative.'"

When World War II clouds began to gather, Einstein studied the dangers of modern weapons. In August, 1939, he warned President Roosevelt about the coming use of atomic energy. But Einstein himself refused to work on the atom bomb for it was a weapon which would destroy people.

In 1945, Einstein retired from his official duties. He made very few public appearances, but when a little girl wrote to him asking for help with her mathematics homework, Einstein replied at once, enclosing the solution to her classroom problem.

On April 18, 1955, when Einstein was 76, death took the great physicist who was also a man of humble heart and deep humanity.

'A LIFE LIVED FOR OTHERS'